MIRELLA D'AMBROSIO SERVODIDIO

THE QUEST FOR HARMONY: THE DIALECTICS OF COMMUNICATION IN THE POETRY OF EUGENIO FLORIT

SOCIETY OF SPANISH AND SPANISH-AMERICAN STUDIES

SSSAS: HF-102 (LC)

(ISBN):   0-89295-008-0
Library of Congress Catalogue Card Number: 78-66111

Printed in the United States of America
Impreso en los Estados Unidos de América

«*Il mio supplizio*
è quando
non mi credo
in armonia.»

Giuseppe Ungaretti, «I fiumi»

TO JOE
--for his devoted support--

TABLE OF CONTENTS

LIST OF TABLES

x

Editions Used and Abbreviations

AP   *Antología penúltima.*   Madrid: Editorial Plenitud,   1970.
     [This anthology incorporates the poetry of *Trópico, Doble
     Acento, Reino, Poema Mío, Asonante Final, Hábito de
     Esperanza* and, the unpublished, «Otros Poemas.»]
DTA *De Tiempo y Agonía (Versos del Hombre Solo].*   Madrid:
     Revista de Occidente, 1974.

CHAPTER I

INTRODUCTION

In a steadfast devotion to his craft that spans a period of more than fifty years, Eugenio Florit has moved within the mainstream of contemporary Spanish poetry, thereby shaping with his opus a remarkable compendium of the divergent poetic configurations of the century. While vibrating empathically with contemporary trends, Florit has headed the beat of his own drum and the result is an interesting confluence of styles arrived at in an unbroken process of experimentation and growth.

The trajectory of his work in its formal aspects, clearly posited by various critics,(1) is one of impressive scope and range and weaves deftly from one school of writing to another in a manner that is alternately successive (postmodernism, vanguardism, neogongorism) and simultaneous (pure poetry, surrealist poetry, traditional poetry) with the adoption of a «confessional» voice marking the poet's arrival at a final plateau. On a *prima facie* basis, then, Florit's poetry appears notably protean and pluralistic in nature. Yet, a careful study of his writings suggests that the seminal concept governing his poetry is one of duality rather than diversity for, despite the varying vestments with which he clothes his verse, the differences of tenor and timbre are more apparential than real. The outer parameters of Florit's cosmos remain poised in dialectical opposition between Classicism and Romanticism, formalism and expressionism, artifice and passion, externally reflective of the polarity which besieges the poet from within and beleaguers him to the end.

The notion of duality as it applies to Eugenio Florit's poetry may be considered from various viewpoints. On one level, and as expressed by Dámaso Alonso in his much cited article, «Escila y Caribdis de la literatura española,» the pull between opposing forces is a permanent characteristic of Spanish literature and, as such, has historic and cultural roots: «Este eterno dualismo

1

dramático del alma española será también ley de unidad de su literatura . . . y es ella --la dualidad misma y no ninguno de los elementos contrapuestos que la forman, considerados por separado-- lo que es peculiarmente español.»(2)   This peculiarly Spanish dualism finds continued expression within contemporary poetry and, indeed, provides an effective framework for numerous studies of this period.   Among these, Ciplijauskaité's «De lo estético a lo humano»(3) and Debicki's «Una generación poética»(4) are especially interesting for the light they shed on a generation of poets whose trajectory is closely linked to Florit's in several important ways.   The duality that typifies the poets of the generation of 1924-25 is summarized by Debicki in the following manner: «. . . la obra lírica de estos poetas revela frecuentemente un conflicto entre dos aspectos del mundo, o entre dos actitudes ante la realidad . . . el doble deseo de ver la poesía como creación de una realidad y como encarnación de valores existentes humanos; el anhelo de seguir al mismo tiempo tradiciones formalistas (la gongorina, la metafórica contemporánea) y tradiciones expresivas (la popular tradicional, la surrealista); el interés simultáneo en la exactitud expresiva y en el misterio de la poesía.»(5)   Divergent perceptions of reality and concomitant differences in poetic expression, elegantly isolated and defined by Amado Alonso in «Clásicos, románticos y superrealistas,» are now in confluence and conflict within a given opus, signposts of a new generation to which Florit adds his voice.

On an existential level, the duality which permeates Florit's poetry is expressive of the tension and polarity intrinsic to human existence when it is viewed as dialectical.   Because the poet's spirit posits itself in a state of disequilibrium, his struggle is one of mediation and integration of the diverse modes in dialectic tension without sacrifice to the distinctions which provide them with articulation and content.   A battle is pitched between the poet's reality as a Kierkegaardian *inter-esse,* a being-between the terms of a contradiction that cannot be resolved but must be resolutely endured,(6) and his longing to realize himself as an *in-dividuum.* Herein does he give tangible expression to the Hegelian conception of spirit not as a simple, self-identical substance but as a dialectical unity of tensed factors.   The notion of polarity thus becomes incorporated with a unitary conception of being.

The classic underpinnings of the concept of polarity provide another dimension for our consideration.   The Pythagorean doctrine that all things are combinations of «opposites,» the Heraclitean conception of the balance of «exchanges,» and the Socratic belief in the reconciliation of «opposites» into a «higher» harmony are useful guideposts to Florit's poetry and lay an important groundwork for understanding and interpretation. In the *Phaedo*, the Hellenic counterpart of the «mystical way» of Christianity, we encounter, perhaps the greatest approximation to those polarities that impact on Florit, e.g. the pull between body and soul, life and death, corruptibility and immutability. Mortality, here, presupposes a two-world interpretation with its very nature a struggle between a higher and lower level.

For Eugenio Florit, this struggle reaches its greatest tension in the extensive body of religious poems which graph his personal *via crucis* and testify to the paradox and contradiction that appear to constitute the very essence of religious experience. As defined by Stace in *Time and Eternity: An Essay in the Philosophy of Religion*, «the religious impulse in men is the hunger for the impossible, the unattainable, the inconceivable--or at least for that which is these things in the world of time.»(7)

In Florit's poetry, then, the notion of polarity, whether understood existentially, Platonically, mystically, or historically, is a seminal one and even receives certification in the titles of two principal collections: the bald acknowledgment of duality in *Doble acento* and the struggle for unity of *Poema mío*.

With the central premise of duality once established, a case must be made for the choice of method for its further study. An exclusively chronological approach has been rejected on the grounds that dialectic tension is operative in all stages of Florit's work. To support the notion of mature serenity advanced by several critics(8) would be to bypass Florit's most recent book, *De tiempo y agonía* (1974), which provides persuasive evidence of continued bifurcations in the poet's path.

A thematic breakdown of the concept of polarity, in all its ramifications, would afford another method of study and would involve the examination of such antithetical categories as ideality and reality, essence and existence, facticity and transcendence--to cite only a few. The danger of this approach is that a «catalogue» of themes does not in itself disclose the locus of the fountainhead from which they flow and which, ultimately, shapes them into a coherent poetic vision. The search for this locus, the encounter and delineation of «el tema vital que desde los adentros preside misteriosamente sobre los demás temas,» as defined by Pedro Salinas,(9) has provided the framework of this study.

From what William James called the «blooming welter of life,» Florit has developed a given set of ideas and attitudes, summarized in recurring symbols, in poetic intuitions, emotions, and doubts, and refined and clarified in a lifetime of effort. They constitute his poetic «universe.» In our judgment, the vital concern that informs this universe, subsuming all other considerations, is the quest for harmony; a quest, implying at its starting point the cognition of a lack, for a harmony equally applicable to an objective state as to a state of mind. The nature of this quest, the emotions that generate it, and their relation to the concept of duality will constitute the body of this study.

Notes

1. The first substantive study of the trajectory of Florit's work is that of Angel del Río in «La literatura de hoy: Eugenio Florit,» *Revista Hispánica Moderna,* New York, Año 8, núm. 3 (1942).   In recent years, the most complete analysis can be found in «La poesía de Eugenio Florit» written by José Olivio Jiménez as a prologue to Alice M. Pollin's *Concordancias de la obra poética de Eugenio Florit.* It also serves as prologue to Florit's *Antología penúltima* (Madrid: Plenitud, 1970).   A trustworthy account of the poet's trajectory may also be found in Orlando E. Saa's book, *La serenidad en la obra de Eugenio Florit* (Miami: Ediciones Universal, 1973).

2. Dámaso Alonso, «Escila y Caribdis de la literatura española,» *Estudios y ensayos gongorinos* (Madrid: Gredos, 1955), pp. 26-27.

3. Biruté Ciplijauskaité, «De lo estético a lo humano,» *El poeta y la poesía* (Madrid: Insula, 1966).

4. Andrew Debicki, «Una generación poética» *Estudios sobre poesía española contemporánea* (Madrid: Gredos, 1966).

5. *Ibid.,* pp. 50-51.

6. Soren Kierkegaard, *Concluding Unscientific Postscript* (Princeton: Princeton University Press, 1944), p. 279.

7. W. T. Stace, *Time and Eternity: An Essay in the Philosophy of Religion* (Princeton: Princeton University Press, 1952), p. 4.

8. Angel del Río, in the aforementioned article of 1942, proclaimed that Florit's «conquista definitiva de la serenidad intelectual» was imminent: in the struggle between disquiet and serenity, «al fin es ésta la que triunfa» (p. 126).   Orlando Saa, in his study of 1973, appears to discount the persuasive evidence of disquiet in Florit's later works and delineates a smooth progression in the poet's writings from spiritual serenity to religious serenity.   Instead, in «La poesía de Eugenio Florit,» José Olivio Jiménez, while stressing the quest for serenity in the poet's work, acknowledges a body of poems that are «más cargadas de humana inquietud.»   The critic again signals out the persistence of this vein of poetry in his prologue to Florit's most recent book, *De tiempo y agonía.*

9. Pedro Salinas, *La poesía de Rubén Darío* (Buenos Aires: Losada, 1948), p. 47.

CHAPTER II

A POETRY OF OUTWARDNESS

The Poet as Exegete: A Doctrine
of Aesthetic Salvation

With the words, «A la serenidad por la inquietud,» Eugenio Florit provides an epigrammatic definition of the nature of his quest and the dialectic process it implies. The poet's «reality» (the spatio-temporal span of his becoming) and his «ideality» (the domain of the intellect and the imagination) are the point and counterpoint of opposing forces in which he is ever caught. The shifting patterns of relationship between these two polarities serve as important indices of the poet's efforts at mediation and, in given instances, point to specific existential choices.

It is with special interest that one turns to the early writings of Florit, for the poetics of «Una hora conmigo» and «Regreso a la serenidad» and the poetry of *Trópico* suggest both in theory and practice the conscious endeavor to subordinate reality to ideality. If, as believed by Kierkegaard, man moves from aesthetic, ethical, and religious spheres of existence, it is the first of these that is most clearly reflected in these writings which, taken together, can be said to provide a doctrine of aesthetic salvation from existential concern.

In view of his sustained engagement with poetry, Florit has been surprisingly sparing where the formulation of a personal poetics is concerned. The only documents available to students of his poetry are «Una hora conmigo» and «Regreso a la serenidad,» both published in 1935.(1) Yet, because so much of Florit's persona is delineated and revealed in these early articles, they are interesting not only for their formulation of the poetics of a specific period, but also for the positioning of pervasive attitudes, hence their continued relevance to students of Florit's poetry today.

«Una hora conmigo» must be viewed, in part, through the prism of the rupture with avantgarde poetry and the enthusiastic rediscovery of Góngora by Florit and his Spanish contemporaries, the poets of the generation of '27. The influence of the Baroque master on the poetry written at this time, though short-lived, is openly acknowledged by Florit.(2) The search for aesthetic purity, the elaboration of a poetic idiom, the organized view of reality, are all lessons learned by Florit from the Cordovan poet and which bear the special imprimatur of his style. Yet, the existential underpinnings of the poetics of «Una hora conmigo» are plain to see and point to a difficult search for harmony that has already begun.

Man, as defined by Heidegger, is «thrown» into a world within which he must work out his destiny. In the face of the uncertainty of the human condition, the desire for orientation becomes a deeply seated human need. In «Una hora conmigo,» Florit appears to equate disharmony with the anarchy and chaos of human reality, passion, and potentiality. Eschewing the risky investment of faith in another being, human or divine, the poet places his belief in a universe of his own creation, subject to his control: «. . . hay que creer en algo. La gente cree en Dios, en el progreso, en el amor. Yo, por ahora, creo en mi poesía, lo cual por otra parte resulta más cómodo que tener fe en los dioses y es menos expuesto al batacazo que suelen llevar los que creen en el amor» (p. 164). Creation, an expression of the poet's ideality, affords him «una valerosa fuga, una ardua evitación de realidades,»(3) a springboard, in Florit's words, to a safer, tidier world, «un mundo suyo, con una perfecta organización, suya también, y una filosofía propia» (p. 166). Here, Florit aligns himself with an entire generation of poets for whom Dámaso Alonso acts as eloquent spokesman: «. . . el mundo nos es un caos y una angustia, y la poesía una frenética búsqueda de ordenación y de ancla.»(4) As defined by José Olivio Jiménez in his penetrating analysis of contemporary poetry, this creative effort expresses «un esfuerzo último y desesperado del hombre por poner un poco de ordenación y claridad en ese caos oscuro y vital de su existencia.»(5)

The psychological need for order, buttressed by stylistic rigor is not achieved without tension and struggle. At the very outset, univocality is displaced by the cognition and the articulation of a «doble acento,» a duality of vision and form: «En mis poemas veréis cosas fijas, claras, de mármol --lo clásico en fin.   Y otras desorbitadas, sin medida, oscuras.   En unas, Goethe o Garcilaso --en otras Walt Whitman o Alberti» (p. 164).   In a manner that is increasingly to become a hallmark of his verse, Florit draws on nature imagery to express his thoughts.   The duality reflective of the poet's inner self is thus revealed, in this article, in a nature that is alternately dark and brooding or serene and numinous: «. . . el día que brilla el sol, y hay cielo azul, y brisa tenue, se escriben cosas de perfecta calma.   Después, a veces ráfagas de misterio, y fuegos fatuos, y gritos en el enrarecido ambiente.   Y el poeta --en este caso yo-- va de sol a tinieblas, de órbita a camino sin ruta, con la antorcha del verso encendida en la mano» (pp. 164-165).   The central fact of dialectic tension and its bearing on style is elaborated further by Florit: by his own confession, the poet alternately controls his verse or is controlled by it.   In the first instance, stylistic constraints, a reflection of the «training formal» to which Florit alludes, perforcedly temper and restrain emotion.   In the second, passions disdain containment, burst through line endings propelling the poet with them: «Pero hay momentos en que toda la fuerza lírica nos sube de quién sabe qué fibra recóndita, no cabe en el verso medido, y hay que verter su esencia en el versículo, en el amplio torbellino de la frase poética, ilimitada y *dejarse arrastrar* [italics mine] por él adonde quiera llevarnos» (p. 165).

Similarly, and in an ontological sense, the poet's definition of the process of «poiesis» suggests the interplay of dual spheres of reality: an external reality defined by him as «mera exposición de la naturaleza» and an internal creative reality given to «mil formas y seres» (p. 167).(6)   This concords with the further distinction made by Florit between «logical» and «poetic» reason. The first offers a systematic appraisal of reality («llama las cosas por su nombre, no fantasea,» (p. 166) while the second exfoliates existential possibilities, offering seeds that flower perennially for the reflective imagination.

The repeated acknowledgment of multileveled dualities in the body of «Una hora conmigo» suggests, then, that while escape from existential concern to an aesthetic sphere stands as an implicit desideratum, it is never fully effected.   While formalism acts as a gateway to harmony, the match between reason and emotion, between ideality and reality still ends in a draw.

In «Regreso a la serenidad,» dialectic differences appear to be suddenly resolved. The poet's arrival at serenity is equated with an unequivocal break with Romanticism and a rediscovery of Classicism. Whether understood existentially as the subjugation of reality to ideality, or seen in a Platonic context as the predominance of two constituent elements of the soul («spirit» and «reason») over the third («appetite»), the fact is that in «Regreso a la serenidad» Florit is unwavering in his support of the classic ideals of equilibrium, reason, proportion, and measure. It remains for us to examine in greater detail what the subscription to Classicism means in the poet's own view and to place this information in a motivational context.

In the first instance, and as noted, the return to Classicism has as its corollary the rejection of the unreasoned egocentrism, the unbridled passion and the license of Romanticism. Yet, the break with Romanticism is more apparential than real, for in the delineation of differences between the two schools, Florit is unwittingly characterizing what are actually or presently divergent impulses in his own work. As clearly perceived by del Río, «Ese clasicismo que podemos llamar romanticismo reprimido, serenidad que pone freno a un ardor y una inquietud latente --es el que persigue Florit.»(7)

In eschewing Romantic poetry, Florit discloses an uneasiness with a reality too close or intense. Averting his glance from the full horizon of life and its multitudinous stirrings, from the complexity of human experience that was allowed to surface in the unrepressed freedom and the dizzying velocity of Romantic and avantgarde poetry, Florit removes himself from life's central arena («. . . el clásico se sabe parte del Universo, no centro. Lleva un movimiento de traslación alrededor de las cosas. Y como está separado de ellas, las ve serenamente y en su tamaño real,» p. 98) and, forthwith, to a safer world («. . . el mundo limitado que tuvo su centro en la filosofía platónica,» p. 103). In the valuing of order and control over impulse, Florit concords with the view held by Juan Ramón Jiménez of the poet's relation to inspiration.(8) The classicist must take as a primary task the shaping of an intelligible and aesthetically satisfying order: «. . . dar forma y norma al mundo actual en el que ya preocupa el coordinar,el asegurar a la razón su papel en el concierto humano y el subordinar los valores a una visión de conjunto» (p. 104); «. . . Tendemos hacia lo abstracto, hacia la organización geométrica, por instinto de unidad, por deseo de equilibrio» (p. 103). For this to be fully accomplished, the floodgates of passion must be firmly closed and emotion must serve as the handmaiden of reason and intelligence: «La inteligencia pretende abarcar hasta los más sutiles estados poéticos. Estos no son, en definitiva, sino concepciones intelectuales desprovistos de toda implicación emotiva» (p. 102). The subordination of the affective and psychic impulses to the conceptual framework of poetry is logicized by the poet in this fashion: «Ya no se agitan 'los invisibles átomos del aire' . . . y aunque ello fuera así, no hallaría resonancia poética en mi corazón, sino en mi pensamiento. . . . Toda una serie de imágenes se dan cita en quién sabe qué circunvolución cerebral para producir lo que llamamos 'hecho poético puro'. . . . La poesía se recoge cada vez más en sí misma, y lo que era en ella delirio de universalidad geográfica, tórnase contemplación de la fuerzas espirituales y expresión comedida en estados intelectuales puros» (p. 102). The intellect, then, is deified and acts as a sturdy barrier against the onslaught of feeling, «los estados del alma que se traducían en el derrame por todos los poros del yo» (p. 103).

Sensorial elements also play a significant role in this poetics for now it is the poet's «eye» (la valorización del sentido plástico,» p. 103) rather than his «I» that records and transmits the poetic message. The poet is perceived by Florit as a dispassionate «observer» of universal harmony and order rather than as «creator» of his own poetic universe: «Crear.   ¿Pero crear, qué? . . . Es empeño romántico el de crear lo que ya está hecho. . . . El toque está en mirar la rosa, el mundo, el poema, con los ojos limpios de telarañas» (p. 100). The poet-observer holds his glance, unwavering, on «Lo actual,» undisturbed by «añoranzas de tiempos pretéritos --romanticismo del recuerdo-- ni ilusiones proyectadas hacia el porvenir» (p. 106). Hence, discord, dissonance, and death («el fetichismo de la muerte,» p. 105) are denied in response to an internal need for harmony: «Ahora vamos adquiriendo un concepto clásico de la vida. Lo que importa es vivirla del mejor modo posible. Hacerla agradable, sana, alegre . . . vivida con serenidad e inteligencia» (p. 105).

While Florit's commitment to Classicism appears unshakable there nonetheless remains an important caveat for the reader for, while the poet can indeed effect a «return to serenity» by embracing classical norms, his ship cannot drop anchor permanently in the Aegean Sea.   «Regreso a la serenidad» becomes more than a manifestation of Florit's concordance with the tenets of «pure poetry,» for in plotting the progression from Romanticism to Classicism, from expressionism to formalism, Florit is, in fact, unconsciously delineating the polar configurations permanently etched in his own work.

Hence the duality openly acknowledged in «Una hora conmigo» or adamantly denied in «Regreso a la serenidad» remains the groundwork of his writing. Both articles share the common impulse to curb reality to ideality. In both, the exaltation of aesthetic control bespeaks intimate knowledge of the existential meaning of its lack.

Trópico: The Delineation of a Cosmos

The direct influence of Góngora, acknowledged in «Una hora conmigo,» and the aesthetic theories postulated in «Regreso a la serenidad» are actively translated into the poetic vision and praxis of Trópico. In this early collection of poems, the poet's subjective reality, his «inwardness,» is domesticated by the intellect and imagination and deflected into a poetry of «outwardness» wherein the unsettling pull of immediate concerns in lessened by the perception of a natural order which surrounds and engulfs them.

What manner of universe Florit fashions for us in Trópico then, accords primarily with the need for an order and control which is best satisfied at this time by withdrawal into formalism where aesthetic constraints, discipline, and rigor become the order of the day. The resulting product is «un trópico en rigurosas y bien contadas décimas(9) . . . el gusto por la metáfora y ciertas reglas de medida y de orden.»(10) The twenty-four décimas of Trópico reveal a poet rarely intrusive, rarely impelled to seek a transaction in which to be personally engaged. Instead we encounter a pure poetry, innocent of any cathartic design, informed and shaped by the intellect alone. Fighting shy of the anecdotal, the narrative or impure, it is a poetry which, as noted by del Río, «se resuelve casi siempre en un medido conceptismo barroco.»(11) The definition of conceptualism as «lo puro, esencial y permanente» put forth by José Olivio Jiménez in Cinco poetas del tiempo is especially applicable to Trópico and stands in contrast to «lo impuro, vivo, cambiante» of a temporal order.(12)

If the poems of Trópico are marked by the search for aesthetic purity, the word «aesthetic» must be understood not only in the traditional sense of pertaining to beauty and the fine arts, but also in the etymological sense of «aisthesis» or sense perception. In both instances the poet achieves the desired subjugation of reality to ideality. In keeping with the objectives articulated in «Regreso a la serenidad» special value is placed on plasticity, on dispassionate reflection of that which lies directly within the poet's field of vision. By elevating the visual imagination above other sense perceptions, the poet creates a «phanopoeia» informed by what the eye can see. The twelve landscapes and the twelve seascapes of *Trópico* are word canvases which establish a direct kinship between poetry and painting and uphold the Horatian dictum expressed two thousand years ago: «Ut pictura, poesis» as the following poems reveal:

> *Realidad de fuego en frío,*
> *quiébrase el sol en cristales*
> *al caer en desiguales*
> *luces sobre el claro río.*
> *Multiplícase el desvío*
> *del fuego solar, y baña*
> *verdes los campos de caña*
> *y jobos de cafetal.*
> *Luego vuelve a su cristal*
> *y en los güines se enmaraña.* (AP, #5, 47)

> *Vuelo de garza en el marco*
> *de tan exigua laguna*
> *que quiebra su luz la luna*
> *en la orilla, como un barco.*
> *Güin osado sale en arco*
> *y apunta a la garza en vuelo;*
> *caen estrellas desde el cielo*
> *a florecer en canciones*
> *y vuelan los corazones*
> *desde la jaula del suelo.* (AP, #9, 49)

For the poet-observer who records the natural scene before him, «la naturaleza es interesante en sí misma.»(13) Yet, as suggested by Blake, the poet sees both *with* and *through* the eye. Far from merely involving elementary sense-awareness, the verses of *Trópico* reveal a collaboration between the eye and

13

the mind's eye, i.e. the response of a mind capable of perception to perceivable objects. A selection process takes place whereby nature is subjected to the poet's ordering intelligence, to the aforementioned desire to «dar forma y norma al mundo actual.»(14) The hyperbolic, exuberant nature of the Cuban tropics is curbed and refashioned in a manner compatible to the poet's need for control. As noted by del Río, «En las imágenes directas el color está siempre mitigado, y los cafetales, los campos de caña, las brisas del mar o las ceibas corpulentas nos dan más bien la impresión de geometrías ordenadas en el paisaje.»(15) However, it is in José Olivio Jiménez' incisive essay, «La poesía de Eugenio Florit,» that the nexus between nature and the poet's quest for harmony as it is reflected in *Trópico* is most clearly perceived: «¿Por qué, primero, un trópico reducido a geometría? Porque el poeta, muy joven aún, teme la conmoción de una naturaleza tropical, exuberante en demasía. Hay que mirarla, sí, y cantarla; pero serenamente: décima, rigor, líneas, giros de la saeta gongorina dominados por la razón emotiva del poeta.   Un trópico estilizado, vivo, pero sentido intelectualmente; pleno de belleza y animación, mas convertido, a la hora del arte, en poesía *serena*. Serena dentro de su mismo movimiento interior, para matizar con exactitud.   El *Trópico* de Florit está a mil años de luz del paisaje romántico y de la naturaleza de América, tal como ha sido vista y cantada (voracidad, desmesura, exuberancia) por los novelistas y aún los poetas de nuestro siglo.»(16)

In *Trópico*, then, Florit commits the infinite variability of nature, visible to the eye, to the limitations and controls imposed by the inner eye. The parameters of this world are carefully drawn with conscious adjustment of visual field to purpose. The desired condition or state which it is the aim of his poetry to reach, is not a splendor that is given whole, but is something presented by Florit in organized glimpses of experience. A geometric reduction of nature is fostered by focusing on discrete units which rarely exceed four and usually number less. Hence the attention, in *Campo* to two elements (the «tibias voces» of dreams and the «trinos de pechos precoces» of dawn, #1, 46), the counterposition of two sounds («eco y cristal,» #2, 46), the focus on one figure («Dulce María,» #3, 47), on three elements («luz,» «monte,» «agua,» #4, 47; «sol,» «río,» «campos,» #5, 47), the recording of a humble occurrence («chirriar del grillo apresado en ruedas de la carreta,» #6, 48), or of a single sound («sale nota del bohío,»

#10, 49).

While the seascapes of *Trópico*, as suggested by del Río, are, in fact, «más conceptuales, más simbólicas, y meditativas,»(17) control is largely retained through a similar restriction of elements which are often interfused in regular patterns. The poet fixes his gaze on surface waters and what the eye can safely see. When overly near or threatening, the dissonant aspects of this natural world are expunged from the poetic record or subsumed by form. In the portrayal of a tropical storm in *Mar* , #8, 53, for example, stylization acts to mitigate the impact of a hostile nature:

> *Castigos de un dios alado*
> *corren sobre el mar, sin freno,*
> *a dividir lo sereno*
> *en pedazos. Azorado*
> *lanza su queja. De lado*
> *van, por agitada cumbre,*
> *sombras en ansia --a la lumbre*
> *escasa de rotos cielos--*
> *tímida de ver sus vuelos*
> *por azul de mansedumbre.*

Or, when viewed from afar, the prospect of a powerful nature is less intimidating: «Vi desde un pico de sierra . . . cómo el cielo se aprestaba/ a caer sobre la tierra» (C, #7, 48).

While *Trópico* has a special underlying ground of exact observation revealed in repeated references to characteristic flora (campos de caña, jobos de cafetal, ceibas, guano, etc.), for the most part, Cuban reality serves only as a thread on which to string a number of rich and colored descriptions that owe as much to the poet's intellect as to his visual acuity. For, the poetry of *Trópico* reveals an uncompromising attempt on Florit's part to give a special view of the world and to produce a special kind of beauty and, consequently, to leave out whatever does not consort with this effort. Yet, the central energizing experience of *Trópico* does rest largely with effects of light and in this sense the poet is faithful to the sundrenched reality of the Cuban tropics: «Realidad de fuego en frío/ quiébrase el sol en cristales. . . . Multiplícase el desvío/ del fuego solar» (C, #5, 47). «Arde el sol y muerde el llano;/ rabia de luz en la tienda . . . agua fresca al mediodía/ para mojar la falsía/ del sol, que abusa en su cumbre./ Sol cuando apagues tu lumbre» (C, #8, 48). «Luciente fuego saldrá/ luego de cegarse inquieto. . . . Ya/ de nuevo rápido va/ mordiendo sendas. Tan duro/ --en el fecundar futuro--/ arquero de flechas rojas» (M, #9, 54). Beyond depicting the candescence of the Cuban sun, Florit paints canvases of light-saturated surfaces and creates shimmering webs of luminosity where the play of light and color often ignore the separateness of objects:

> *Brillan luces voladoras*
> *tan sueltas sobre la casa,*
> *como luminosa masa*
> *partida en tenues auroras.*
> *Entre las brisas sonoras*
> *son átomos de diamante.*
> *Alza un brazo el caminante*
> *al cruzar por la arboleda*
> *y presa en la mano queda*
> *una chispa titilante.* (C, #11, 50)

> *Viaje en descenso feliz*
> *para un resbalar de luz*
> *sobre la mar, al trasluz*
> *quintaesenciado matiz . . .* (M, #3, 52)

> *. . . quiebra su luz la luna*
> *en la orilla, como un barco . . .* (C, #9, 49)

> *...Alegre, al fin, a la cierta*
> *siembra de luces del día.* (M, #1, 51)

> *Mar, con el oro metido. . . .*
> *Viven en cálido nido*
> *aves de tu luz, inquietas . . .* (M, #4, 52)

> *¡Si vinieras tantas veces*
> *cuantas en luceros brillas!*
> *¡Si en luces de maravillas*
> *como en inquietud floreces! . . .* (M, #11,55)

> *...Nubes de color de guerra*

con fuego en las entrañas. . . (C, #7, 48)

Lyric themes of sea and field are worked, with stylized diction, into a framework of substantial complexity. The metaphorical underlay of some of the *décimas* creates a background and middle distance to which the eye is continually being carried. In *décima* #2 of *Campo*, Florit reveals himself to be as much a poet of the ear as of the eye. Here, as in #4, the continual shifting of the inner eye, of the ear and the mind produces a special kind of beauty:

> *Eco y cristal vienen juntos*
> *hasta la falda del monte.*
> *Voz de escondido sinsonte*
> *y de caudales presuntos*
> *aprisionan en dos puntos*
> *un silencio de mañana.*
> *Eco gira por la vana*
> *concreción de la maleza*
> *y el cristal, ya río, empieza*
> *a dividir su sabana.* (C, #2, 46)

> *Húndese la luz inquieta*
> *para abrirle unas pupilas*
> *y pueda el monte tranquilas*
> *horas mirar por su grieta,*
> *El agua, entonces sujeta,*
> *rasga pretéritos lazos;*
> *y al saltar hecha pedazos*
> *de fresca cristalería.*
> *condensa la luz del día*
> *con la sombra entre sus brazos.* (C, #4, 47)

The elaboration of a «purer» idiom, free from daily contamination, is in part effected by a metaphoric labeling of nature which frequently involves the conversion of adjectives into substantives. The most common of these is the use of *cristal* to designate water («cristal,» C, #2, 46; «cristalería,» C, #4, 47; «cristales,» «cristal,» C, #5, 47), and *fuego* and *oro* to depict the sun («fuego,» C, #5, 47, M, #9, 54; «oro,» M, #4, 52). The many enjambements, the use of synesthesia («el cantar dorado,» C, #1, 46), the latinized word order, all allow Florit to cast his verse in a mold less affected by ordinary habits and rhythms of speech as, for example, with the inversion, «Náufrago suspiro tanto» of Mar, #12, 55. Again, in *décima* #5, 47, of *Campo*, by breaking the normal syntactic order, Florit maximizes the desired effect of color and plasticity: «Multiplícase el desvío/ del fuego solar y baña/ verdes los campos de caña.»   The personification of nature, perhaps the most frequently employed trope, becomes a highly expressive stylistic device in Florit's hands:

> ...Nubes de color de guerra
> con fuegos en las entrañas
> hundían manos extrañas
> en las ceibas corpulentas ... (C, #7, 48)

> Arde el sol y muerde el llano... (C, #8, 48)

> ... por anhelo de ser nada
> en marina cárcel preso,
> ábrese suicida beso
> de nube en sendas oscuras ... (M, #5, 52)

> Húndese la luz inquieta
> para abrirle unas pupilas
> y pueda el monte tranquilas
> horas mirar por su grieta ... (C, #4. 47)

> Flecha en un éxtasis verde,
> ilusionada en su altura,
> contempla la tierra dura
> y en un suspiro se pierde.
> Se empina a la luna y muerde
> nácar azul de verano;
> lo derrama sobre el llano
> con pinceles de destreza
> y se tiñe la cabeza
> con seda de luna en guano. (C, #12, 50)

A pattern of antithesis, which also contributes to the *culto* tone of *Trópico*, reveals a complex mind and sensibility behind the poetry:

Hoy, en voces de la ausencia,
lejos (*A*) *de tí, por mirarte*
cerca (*A*) *llega de tu parte*
milagro fiel de tu esencia . . . (M, #7, 53)

Llanto risueño (*A*), *y el* llanto
medroso (*A*) *de lejanías . . .* (M, #12, 55)

Flecha en éxtasis verde, (*A*)
ilusionada en su altura (*B*)
contempla la tierra dura (*B*)
y en un suspiro se pierde (*A*) . . . (C, #12, 50)

Arde el sol (*A*) *y muerde el* llano (*B*) . . .
Sombra (*A*) *de* río (*B*) *y de guano . . .* (C, #8, 48-49)

Voz (*A*) *de escondido sinsonte*
y de caudales presuntos
aprisionan en dos puntos
un silencio (*A*) *de mañana . . .* (C, #2, 46)

Por el sueño (*A*) *hay tibias voces. . . .*
Trinos de pechos precoces
inquietos al despertar (*A*) . . . (C, #1, 46)

As a practitioner of pure poetry, Florit reflects the desired nature of things in the architecture of his poems, in the attention to proportion, measure, and balance, in the careful arrangement of images and metaphors, silences and sounds. The sense of organization of this poetry is heightened by the election of the *décima* with its fixed recurrences and consonant rhyme and its carefully prescribed length which can only hold small parcels of reality at a time. The complementarity of structural and perceptual control stands as the *sine qua non* of the poet's efforts to shape a cosmos.

Yet, even within the controlled world of Florit's *Trópico*, lurking below the surface are feelings despairing of containment. Pivotal themes, foreshadowing existential battles yet to be waged, are already intimated: the poet's solitude («con mi soledad estaba,» C, #7, 48); the dialectic pull of opposing forces («y vuelan los corazones/ desde la jaula del suelo,» C, #9, 49); disquiet at time's passage («La fuga de mis días,» M, #12, 55). Yet, because they are disengaged from any anecdotal circumstance affording definition or context, a detached overview is maintained and the poet, retaining control, remains the consummate artificer of form. In this poetry of outwardness, therefore, Florit's reality is largely submerged and the resulting harmony, though it be achieved by the ascendancy of reason over desire,(18) appears genuine.

Notes

1.   «Una hora conmigo,» *Revista Cubana,* VII, núms. 4, 5, 6 (1935) 159-167; «Regreso a la serenidad,» *Universidad de la Habana,* Año III, núms. 8-9 (marzo-junio, 1935) 97-108.

2.   In «Una hora conmigo,» Florit expounds on the influence of Góngora: «¿qué significa tal énfasis del gongorismo? . . . Fue como quien echa a andar bajo el sol de agosto, por un camino abierto a todas las saetas luminosas, y halla, de pronto, el árbol grato a cuya sombra se enjuga el sudor y se goza la brisa.   Por eso, los poetas de habla castellana, que habíamos probado que sabíamos y podíamos ser libres, nos juntamos un día a la sombra del roble gongorino para hacer ejercicios de humildad,» p. 162.

3.   These words are attributed by Florit to Ortega in «Una hora conmigo,» p. 166.

4.   Dámaso Alonso, *Poetas españoles contemporáneos* (Madrid: Gredos, 1958), p. 57.

5.   José Olivio Jiménez, *Cinco poetas del tiempo* (Madrid: Insula, 1964), p. 57.

6.   Similarly, and as analyzed by Debicki in *Estudios sobre poesía española contemporánea,* there appear to be two governing concepts of poetry in the generation of 1924-1925:   «. . . el de la poesía como creación de algo nuevo a base de materiales reales transformados y el de la poesía como descubrimiento y comunicación de lo real,» p. 23.

7.   Angel del Río, «La literatura de hoy: Eugenio Florit,» *Revista Hispanica Moderna,* Año 8, núm. 3 (1942), p. 214.

8.   Biruté Ciplijauskaité describes Juan Ramón Jiménez' thoughts in this fashion: «[El poeta] No quiere galopar ciegamente montado en la inspiración.   Lo ideal es dominar esta fuerza y depurarla.   No entregarse a la imaginación sino ordenarla.» *El poeta y la poesía* (Madrid: Insula, 1966), p. 195.

9.   This quotation is attributed by Florit to Alfonso Reyes in «Una hora conmigo,» p. 162.

10.   Eugenio Florit, «Una hora conmigo,» p. 163.

11.   Angel del Río, p. 210.

12.   José Olivio Jiménez, *Cinco poetas del tiempo,* p. 23.

13.   Eugenio Florit, «Regreso a la serenidad,» p. 101.

14.   *Ibid.,* p. 104.

15.   Angel del Río, p. 209.

16.   José Olivio Jiménez, «La poesía de Eugenio Florit,» prologue to *Antología penúltima,* p. 38.

17.   Angel del Río, p. 210.

18.   Plato takes man to be a synthesis of reason and appetite, with «spirit» merely as the togetherness that unites the other two.   As seen, the harmony experienced by Florit in this early stage of his life is won at the expense of this Platonic synthesis or balance of parts.

CHAPTER III

A POETRY OF INWARDNESS: THE ANATOMY OF DISQUIET

The reader soon discovers that the explicitly cerebral dimension of understanding of Florit's poetry is no more than the uppermost tip of the iceberg.   The cosmos fashioned by the poet in *Trópico* is soon shaken by internal commotions with emotion the «fault» cutting down to the bedrock of hidden feeling.   Florit comes to feel the need to understand himself and the world not simply with his mind but with his entire being.

Dámaso Alonso's cogent analysis of the direction taken in poetry in the years ranging between 1920 and 1936 is peculiarly applicable to the work of Eugenio Florit: «[La poesía].   Salío a la vida como llena de pudores, con limitación de temas, con un miedo de expresar la pasión, con un sacro horror a lo demasiado humano, con muchas preocupaciones técnicas, con mucho miedo a las impurezas, desdén de lo sentimental.   Pero en aquellos mismos versos escarbando un poco se encontraba la pasión que se quería ocultar.   Por muchas causas, por un entrecruzamiento de cana-lillas, como bella inundación irrumpe la vida (27-36) y la poesía que no con entera razón se había tildado de poco humana, termina siendo apasionada, llena de ternura, y no pocas veces frené-tica.»(1)

In the poetry of *Doble acento,* it is already evident that emotions can shake the foundations of the most elegant intel-lectual edifice.   While from the poet's point of view, the struggle to maintain control at this time meets with alternations of success and failure, poetically he has never been more interesting, moving easily from the clear accents of «pure poetry» to the sweep and opacity of «surrealism.»

In later collections, as feelings continue to surface and are openly acknowledged, the poet's own inwardness becomes the central reality with which he is properly occupied--a reality to which he has entrance without trespass.   Yet, «inwardness» does not connote «mindlessness.» Having granted recognition to emotion, Florit can direct his reason to the arduous task ahead-- that of seeking to integrate the elements of personality into the unity of person. Like the Kierkegaardian ethical man, the poet must take his given nature in hand and make it his own responsibility.

In «Biografía» (AP, 353), an insightful and incisive self-portrait written in 1968, Florit succeeds in isolating and defining those pervasive feelings which constitute the principal themes of his opus. They deal, *grosso modo,* with love, death, and time.

> *Ya cumplió sus sesenta y cinco años.*
> *Ha amado mucho, pocas veces. . . .*
> *Aún ama mucho.   El sol, los árboles,*
> *las primaveras, los inviernos.   Su casa sola*
> *y sus recuerdos.*
> *Aún ama mucho. . . .*
> > *Cuando muera*
> *--ojalá que no sea muy pronto--*
> *dirán de él: fue un hombre bueno.*
> *Tal vez dirán: un poco ingenuo.*
> *Y acaso digan: amó mucho.*
> *Por lo mucho que amó, Dios lo perdone.*

Emphasis on love, conveyed through repetition, permeates the first stanza which also outlines the direction this emotion takes: human love («Ha amado mucho, pocas veces»); nature («el sol, los árboles, las primaveras, los inviernos»); the poet's memories and his solitude («Una casa sola, sus recuerdos»). The twice-repeated «Aún ama mucho,» in transition from «Ha amado mucho» seeks, through bald assertion to confirm a vitality subconsciously held in doubt. We are not prepared for the abrupt transition of Stanza III. The calculated brevity of the first verse, «Cuando muera,» offset typographically for further effect, jolts us into an awareness of death's inevitability despite the warming assertions of Stanza I. And, caught between love (referred to again in Stanza II) and death, is the unremitting passage of time-never stated but effectively intimated in the progression of tenses:

Ya cumplío *sus sesenta y cinco años*

(Preterite: notion of completed time; awareness of finitude)

Ha amado *mucho, pocas veces* . . .

(Present perfect: sixty-five years are but yesterday; the contingency of time)

Aún ama *mucho, el sol, los árboles,*

(The poet anchors himself in the present tense: the struggle for affirmation)

la primavera, *los* inviernos. *Su casa sola*

(the seasons as metaphors for time's passage)

Y sus recuerdos

(Past made present through evocation)

Aún ama *mucho*

(Reaffirmation of the present, of life)

Cuando muera
Ojalá que no sea muy pronto
dirán *de él:* fue *un hombre bueno*

(The juxtaposition of the indefinite future and the future of probability with the preterite tense, suggesting the simultaneity of completion or closure. The inability to experience the present free of reflection on time's contingency)

Tal vez dirán: *un poco ingenuo*
Y acaso digan: amó *mucho*
Por lo mucho que amó, *Dios lo* perdone

The poet as he sees himself is very much as he gives himself to us in his work. Allowing him, then, to guide us, we can confidently embark on a consideration of the nature and character of feelings experienced and expressed in Florit's poetry of inwardness, and their relation to his central quest.

Eros as the Tendance of the Body

Eros as the craving or desirous love of something which is its correlate has both erotic and spiritual motivation in the writings of Eugenio Florit. Here we will concern ourselves with Eros as it regards the tendance of the body, reserving the study of the spiritual projection of Eros for a later section.

Florit's poetry is undoubtedly marked by temperance and control over physical appetition. During long stretches of time he succeeds, with remarkable restraint, in concealing the depth and intensity of the feelings of which he is capable. Disclosures are often made begrudgingly and by indirection. Loss of composure on the part of the poet is rarely suffered as emotions are mostly examined retrospectively, having already been dominated or restrained. Yet, despite the safeguards imposed by the poet, erotic feelings will have out. While the reader must, in some instances, be disposed to meet the poet halfway, what he ultimately encounters is not jejune sentimentality but full-bodied passion.

Two approaches to Eros seem to prevail. The first one involves veiled reference or indirection: by telling us what he is *not* presently experiencing, the poet affords us a glimpse of unbridled desires of the past: «Sin el ardor lascivo. . . . Qué lejana la voz de los amores» (AP, 88). «Lúbrico ayer con las manos trementes/ a cada alzar de una cálida voz» (AP, 96). «. . . lo que hace un momento lo tenía/ fuera de sí» (AP, 345). «Amor ya sin acento» (AP, 77). Though vulnerability to love is sometimes openly confessed, the impact of such revelation is frequently mitigated by poetic diction and voice, as with the whimsical simplicity of several «Canciones para la soledad» (AP, 181-87):

> *Amor tú sí tendrías*
> *dulce el hablar y la caricia suave. . .* (#5)

> *¿Adónde vas, amor?*

No, no me lo digas.
Déjame en el temblor
de mis orillas.

Pero sí; ¿adónde vas?
¿Para qué callas? . . . (#12)

Soñador de sueños: abre
al nuevo amor los balcones . . .(#16)

Nada se ha muerto.   Nada.
¡Si hasta el amor lo estoy sintiendo
entre las soledades de mi alma! (#11)

For the most part, however, Eros in Florit's poetry is seen from the perspective of loss and pain of want.   In turn, this perspective receives a two-pronged projection hinging on the immediacy or distance of the emotional breakpoint.

In «Preludio» (AP, 206), the poet's resolve to acknowledge passion («Quiero pensarte,/ noche de silenciosa espera») is reached only after experiencing perturbation at the very prospect of remembrance: «Se recuerda el ayer . . . con un temor de hundir el pensamiento/ en corola de flor; como, a la noche,/ un miedo de soñar con lo imposible/ que nos hará llorar después, despiertos.»   However, the poet makes brave to confront the love-episode which, viewed retrospectively, serves to infuse with gentled light, the darkness of his horizon: «Ahora, sin amor, vienen las ondas/ del mar aquel al hombre y su destino;/ y a su serena luz, qué plácida/ la senda entre las sombras aparece.»   While the primacy of love is affirmed («primero es el amor») and thrice repeated, distance and time have transformed passion into tender remembrance called forth by a «gris recuerdo.»   The stylized and metaphoric description of the lover's «sueño de amor» and the carefully orchestrated treatment of nature suggest the idealization and embellishment of past reality.   The poet's memory is selective, circumventing the painful circumstance of separation and sorting out from this past only the enduring gifts of Eros.   Eros-recalled, then, becomes Eros-transformed with gratitude as the keynote of the poem:

. . . Por el día

que abrió su flor el mundo de mis sueños
a la naciente claridad del alma;
por la ternura que me diste;
por este gris recuerdo
que entre las sombras con su dardo hiere;
por la eterna ilusión que sobre el viento
dejaste para fuente de mi vida:
como primero fue el Amor, primero
en noche y ruiseñor estás conmigo
y en ruiseñor y noche me acompañas.

«Nocturno III,» #3 (AP, 116), cushioned neither by illusions nor arabesques of style, focuses sharply on the reality of solitude itself:

Mi corazón para tu noche, noche;
que lo dejaron solo, sordo, ciego,
fantasma ya de antiguos corazones,
niebla de flor en tu callado centro.

The use of the impersonal form («lo dejaron solo») illustrates the poet's method of dealing with his feelings through abstraction of the love agent inflicting pain.   Yet, the personification of the poet's heart which, through loss, becomes «unhearing» and «unseeing» attests to his realizaton that emotions impinge on perception.

    In «Soledad» (AP, 97), the same senses are again effected. With the epigraph («Por la oscura región de vuestro olvido»-- Garcilaso) as index to the circumstances triggering the writer's solitude, his incompletion finds eloquent expression.   The conceit formulated by Aristophanes in the *Symposium* which suggests that each man is but half a complete creature in passionate search of his other half is converted, here, into moving truth.   In the absence of his «complement,» a love-partner with whom to «coalesce,» the poet's very reality appears in doubt: «Para sentirme vivo echo al viento mi nombre. . . .   Soledad a los vientos por regiones oscuras,/ con la mirada ausente, y una tímida angustia/ de asomarme a las aguas, y no ver mi figura,/ y atravesar las noches con el alma desnuda.»   Yet, while the poet's solitude is made patently clear, one notes in the body of the poem a lack of specification, a disengagement of emotion from kindling circumstance characteristic of the approach to Eros through indirection.

In «Soneto,» #7 (AP, 88), memory again acts as a link to Eros. However, unlike the abstractions, the discreet wistfulness of the poems already discussed, the full force of the poet's feelings remains unchecked suggesting a more proximate love episode. With the first four verses of the sonnet's octave, a climate of anguish and pain is established through qualification, comparison, and personification

> *Sobre la* espina *del recuerdo llega*
> *a* gritarme *tu voz* desesperada,
> *como una mariposa* deshojada
> *entre* las manos de la noche ciega . . .

Depth of feeling can be further plumbed in the sonnet's sextet where, in the circumstance of loss or estrangement, the poet portrays himself as beyond pain by virtue of its very intensity:

> *No me hiere el ardor, de tan profundo;*
> *de tan grave, no duele el pensamiento;*
> *no corre, de tan firme, este segundo*

> *que viene alado al pie del firmamento,*
> *Agua de paz para mi seco mundo*
> *metido en un rincón de su aposento.*

Among the most powerful and revealing of the love poems expressing recent loss is «Nocturno II» (AP, 112). Employing free verse, the poet allows his feelings to spill over, uncontained and unmasked. The specificity of circumstantial detail volunteered («. . . el remordimiento de tu partida inútil . . . los yelos de tu olvido . . . tu engaño . . . estos clavos de anhelos . . .») and the externalization of subterranean feelings of anguish, regret, fear, and loneliness further attest to the poet's candor. Solitude, through loss, is forcefully intuited and depicted as a subconscious reversion to the helpless vulnerability of childhood («me sentí como un niño, solo en mitad de la selva/ caliente . . .»). Correspondingly, fear is expressed primitively and in a manner appropriate to the child («echaba a rodar mi grito») yet with none of the release of tension provided by the primal scream («lo veía

tornar a mí, rotas las alas, a hundir el pico en mi garganta . . .»).
Essentially, the poem juxtaposes the poet's dream state with his
waking state, thereby affording us a singular view of the interplay
of antithetical perceptions and perspectives. Dreams, wrought in
the soothing dark of night, anchor the poet to his past and to
memories of love («. . . me suben desde el fondo del sueño tus
manos con una/ esencia de violetas de nieve;/ y todo el sabor
inquieto que destiló tu boca . . .»). Wakefulness signifies the
emptiness of the present, the reality of the poet's solitude ushered
in by the harsh light of day, i.e. the light of truth («me espanta la
claridad que va llegando . . . esa triste claridad . . . como me
duelen tanto las espinas del alba . . .»). Through psychological
projection, nature mirrors the poet's internal disharmony:

> . . . cuando se sabe que ya no hay otra cosa que esperar más
> que la muerte de los árboles . . .
> No me imagino el mundo sino después de haber sentido
> entre los dedos los esqueletos de las hojas
> cuando se ponen a llorar bajo la luna por la caricia de los
> pájaros . . .
> Por el camino caminar sin ver qué nubes cantan la
> ausencia de la luz;
> porque hasta ayer nada más tenía el mundo un destino de
> morir en tus ojos . . .

Though erotic passion, here, is already once removed, the poet's
feelings are too oppressive to bear even retrospectively. Before
he can regain his calm, all traces of the love-episode must be
erased from the wellspring of memory:

> . . . Pero no quiero saber la pobre fiesta de canciones
> desnudas;
> no, no quiero tu engaño desde el mar ni la compasión de
> tantas azucenas
> cuando estoy aquí solo, con el olvido de las lágrimas,
> hundido tu recuerdo entre las manos para sembarlo lejos
> de mi, por las auroras infinitas.

More important than this final resolution itself is the nature of
the feelings that generate it. By allowing them to surface in all

30

their savage intensity, the poet affords us a rare glimpse of the fever of his heart, of a moment in his life profoundly touched by the welterings of passion.

Among Florit's most intense love poems are those which appear in «Otros poemas» (AP, written in 1966 and 1967). «Solo, lejos de tí» (347), «Vuelvo a encontrarme» (349), «Poesía, sí» (350), «Nadie conversa contigo» (350), quintessential love poems all, are united by a common them: the death of the poet's beloved. Dispelling any vestige of doubt that Eros is bypassed by Logos, they unequivocally give the lie to the reasoned utterances of «Una hora conmigo» or «Regreso a la serenidad.»

Impatient of all intellection and abstraction, in this body of poems the poet discloses his feelings at their rawest. The loss of the «other» is experienced viscerally, felt in the blood («como una espina/ clavada entre los ríos más hondos de mi sangre»). The inconsolable grief of the «one» («hundido,» «perdido,» «desvalido[s],» «. . . sin ecos que respondan, sin otros ojos que los míos . . .») wrap these verses in a climate of directionless despair. Spatial imagery, repetition, and antithesis become effective devices counterposing reality and desire, inwardness and outwardness («vuelvo *a encontrarme* [A] *donde* [B] *ya* [C] *no estás* [D] . . . *a no encontrarme* [A] . . . *Afuera* [B] el *sol* [E]. . . . Pero *aquí* [B] *ya* [C] *no estás* [D] ... busco en la *sombra* [E]/ de *este rincón* [B] callado, y *no te encuentro* [A] ...»). Disconnected from the outside world by the boundaries of his pain, the poet is indifferent to the call and stir of a life which, viewed nihilistically, becomes a «melancólico no . . . una terca negación» within a barren horizon («días sin luz . . . estrellas muertas . . . el otoño con sus tristes hojas . . . cansadas . . . se deshacen . . . un cielo sin color . . .»). The poet's painful solitude becomes exacerbated rather than mitigated by time's passage: «Nadie conversa contigo/ más que el tiempo del reloj./ Soledad de sones íntimos,/ llena de sordo clamor. . . . (AP, 351). Aún más solo que ayer, y menos que mañana, que ha de traerme un grano más de tierra/ para la semilla de muerte que me habita . . .» (AP, 347). In a present absent of meaning and a future offering no hope, the poet denies the flow of time by anchoring himself in a past that carries with it the solace of memory «¿Y qué hacer sino regresar al recuerdo,/ o perderme en el bosque donde los árboles se nutren de tu forma/ y la yerba que piso me repite tu nombre? . . . (AP, 347)/ Con la memoria de la voz que un día/ supo llenar mi soledad, y que hoy me duele. . . . (AP, 349) El alma vaga prendida/ al recuerdo de una voz . . .» (AP, 351). Written under the impact of recent loss, these poems carry a special urgency and authenticity. Harmony through love appears to stand beyond human achievement, thwarted by irrational events that ever remind the poet of the natural, mortal, and vital side of existence.

In the poems of *De tiempo y agonía,* produced between 1970-72, Eros continues to be portrayed through the prism of loss of unity understood Platonically. Hunger for completion, harmony, and wholeness, is the principal configuration of Eros in this collection. The generating circumstance of these love poems (loss of the beloved) yokes them to the preceding group. The acute pitch of the earlier poems is now tempered; yet, the poet passively submits to the same absence of hope, the same numbed routinization which again provides a safe if barren retreat. The push and pull of natural forces, once censored by reason, are now thwarted by withdrawal and alienation: «Leo, pinto, escucho música/ a veces escribo versos. . . . Algún día me siento vivo/ y otros, los más, como si muerto . . . ya sin temores ni esperanzas . . .»(29) Yet, stasis and calm are but imperfect mechanisms of self defense. They are repeatedly shattered by yearnings that surface with abrupt intensity, by sudden glimpses of the desolation of the poet's «corazón deshecho.» (45) The confrontations of the poet with his feelings are most often sparked by an awareness of love's presence about him. Seeing the union of others, by antithesis he suffers his own incompletion:

> . . . *Miro pasar, de mi ventana,*
> *las parejas de pelos sueltos,*
> *con las cinturas enlazadas*
> *y pasos iguales y lentos . . .*
> («El olvidado,» p. 29)

> . . . *¿La mirada que sale sin destino*
> *de amor, sin esperanza*
> *de la otra mirada que la encuentre? . . .*
> («El aire triste,» p. 59)

> . . . *El hombre solo*
> *no gusta de los días que se alargan,*
> *como su afán, en horas luminosas.*

Luz para el joven, besos en la esquina,
juntas las manos y las almas . . .
    («Elegía en primavera,» p. 49)

The disengagement and passivity evidenced in numerous poems is as often a shield against hope as it is against sorrow. Yet, ultimately the poet surrenders his arms to Eros and acknowledges feelings that have been denied.   Still, in several poems, as if reluctant to enter life's arena anew, Florit fights shy of specificity and clothes his desires in abstractions.   («Que, lo que espero con ansia/ es sólo un sueño./ Un fantasma de amor único/ que no es cierto,» (39); «. . . Amo lo que no se acerca,» (29); «. . . Y en el sueño, el amor a quien no existe . . . este afán de querer, de amar lo que no se tiene,» (43-44).   Yet, other poems find the poet disposed to greater specification and autobiographical focus.   «Nosotros» (47), for example, clearly plots Florit's trajectory from «nosotros» to «el solo yo» to «la espera de nosotros.»   In the intense yearning for a love partner, and in the portrayal of Eros as triumphant over Thanatos, «Nosotros» closely echoes the hypothetical question of Hephaestus as phrased in the *Symposium:* «Do you desire to be wholly one; always day and night to be in one another's company?   For, if this is what you desire, I am ready to melt you in one and let you grow together, as that being two you shall become one, and while you live, live a common life as if you were a single man, and after your death in the world below still be one departed instead of two.»(2)

Poder decir nosotros siempre.
Decir estamos, vamos, vemos, iremos, fuimos, volveremos.
Todos los verbos de dos, como juntas las manos.
Saber lo otro por lo nuestro.
Lo uno por lo del otro.
El tiempo pasa al lado sin angustia.
Pasa el sol, las nubes pasan y nosotros las miran.
Esos nosotros piensan a la vez una cosa
y es ello lo que une como un hilo invisible.
A veces el espacio separa, separa hasta la muerte.
Pero es siempre nosotros.
Luego es el yo, el solo yo.   La espera del nosotros.
Un nosotros que todo lo venza: hasta la muerte.

Out of the fragmentary search of the self within the self, wholeness and with it harmony can be newly achieved. From his lovelorn condition, Florit struggles for reaffirmation and allows himself to pass anew from a state of «being» to «becoming» («Aunque, después de todo, hay que seguir,» 50). However, for a new porosity to become effective, the poet must first deal positively with the past. The stylized manner and diction notwithstanding, in the poem «A la manera de Jorge de Montemayor,» (51), the hold of the past on the present is clearly conveyed.

> ¡Quién bebiera, Felicia, el agua clara
> con que el amor conviertes en olvido!
> ¡Quién, por no revivir lo ya vivido,
> al placer del recuerdo renunciara!
>   ¡Quién, Felicia, a tu fuente se acercara
> para limpiar el sueño estremecido
> que jamás, ni despierto ni dormido,
> logra borrar la imagen de su cara!
>   Pero si es bien que el daño no se evite,
> y noche y día el corazón palpite
> al dulce resonar del nombre amado,
> no me des a beber esa agua pura
> para poder llorar al bien pasado,
> Felicia, en tanto que la vida dura.

The force of Eros, concentrated in a relationship once removed must be disentangled from sorrow for the memory of the loved one to be safely exalted and nurtured. Then, though past love be cherished the poet is free to redirect the present and to answer to a heart that «aún arde constante» (p. 64). That the unremitting pull of Eros ultimately prevails is made clear in «Homenaje a Quevedo» (p. 63). While the poem is a pastiche of verses drawn directly from the Baroque master, the manner and order in which they are assembled are as revealing of the borrower as of the creator. Here, Eros is seen as dialectician mediating between passion and the intellect. While in the second stanza this dichotimization is posited as the poet's burden, the final accent falls emphatically on the word «enamorado»:

> Dióme el cielo el amor, dióme la vida

> *que a la muerte me lleva despeñado;*
> *y entre mi pensamiento y mi deseo*
> *cargado voy de mí, y enamorado . . .*

The cravings of the heart accompany him to the end, freed only with the passage into death («pienso que he de vivir cuando me muera,/ libre ya de pasión y sentimiento . . .»).

A final review of Eros as the tendance of the body suggests the following trajectory. In an initial and prolonged phase which carries the reader to *Hábito de esperanza*, Eros appears fleetingly and almost always by indirection. If it escapes concealment, it is placed at a safe distance, stylized or abstracted. Eroticism and sensualism are absent, for while Florit perforce recognizes himself as a part of nature and therefore, to a degree, bound by his senses, he maintains control by withholding consent: he becomes master over himself, in nature and outside. The reader is afforded only occasional glimpses of feeling that suggest an existential engagement with love, a surrender to the flux of experience and to the blind thrusts of fate.

However, in «Otros poemas» and *De tiempo y agonía,* sorrow in love becomes the springboard for increased candor. While Eros shares in the nature of both parents, Poros and Penia, abundance and poverty, in this phase of Florit's writing it is clearly the latter attribute that prevails. When viewed through the prism of poverty (understood as the loss of the love partner) Eros reveals its fullest force and meaning to the reader. The poet's subsequent solitude alternately carries enshrinement of the past love experience or hope of renewal. However, in this final stage, whether Eros is viewed elegiacally or through reaffirmation, the touchstone of harmony is clearly the unity of the «self» with the «other.»

Thanatos

In the body of poems to be studied under this rubric, the poet, caught in the toil of time, particularity, and finitude, stands before the fact of his own existence and gives voice to anxieties and concerns which clamor for recognition. Emotion is not susceptible, here, to dismissal as a corruptive force nor to subjugation by the laws of reason. For, the poet knows himself bound in the temporal process («Dióme el cielo . . . la vida/ que a la muerte me lleva despeñado,» DTA, 63) and his response to his finitude is intensely agonic. As if from the abyss of feeling and sentiency, of raw openness to the world, out of the dark and secret wells of his aloneness, a knowledge of his mutability has gathered and broken. Moving from varying higher and lower levels of insight, the poet's experience unfolds in the disclosure of deeper meaning. In shuddering response to the sheer factuality of the human situation, Florit delineates the gap between time and eternity, the actual and the ideal, life--with its constant reminders of the running down of the body--and creative sensitivity which strives to reach beyond its transient history.

While some poems in the group to be studied record and reflect time from a socio-historic perspective, the principal configuration of this theme is one of personal struggle intensely waged and testimonially recorded. Herein lies the relevance of the following judgment proferred by José Olivio Jiménez: «Las distintas concepciones temporalistas de nuesta época coinciden en proclamar la superior vigencia de un tiempo finito, sujetivo, vivencial, definido en torno a la individualidad de la existencia.»(3)

Time as a Courier of Death

In normal response to the uncertainty of the human condition, Florit experiences feelings of anxiety. Standing between birth and death, with both past and future as constitutive elements of his essential being, the poet must embark on life's journey choosing and shaping his own destiny. The burden of responsibility which rests with the poet is depicted metaphorically in «La sombra» (AP, 189). A sense of life's trajectory and travail is compressed into fifteen verses which stress man's struggle with the «shadow» of life:

> . . . La sombra que precede es más terrible
> que la que no se ve.   La vamos empujando
> y se pega a los pies, y alarga el cuerpo
> que va a romperse en el ocaso. . . .
> Y cuando ya no puede más el cuerpo, quiebra
> su figura en la arena, derrotado,
> para que así la sombra ya no sea
> más que una mancha inerte de dolor en la tarde.

Isolated with the problems, pains, and prospects of his own person, the poet recognizes that he must make a truth for himself. In «Canción de agua y viento» (AP, 75), the terrible existential burden of freedom is likened to the protean sea, unlimited in shape, form and color. Yet, the freedom essential to selfhood is viewed with some cynicism for, like the drops of moisture in the air, man's dreams are destined to evaporate. («... y es un dolor que punza fiero/ saberse libre y estar mirando, como alfileres/ las gotas de cada ensueño sobre la mano...»).

Frequently, the poet expresses conscious awareness of the concrete limiting factors that circumscribe the exercise of choice in life's process. Like the conch in the poem of the same name, «La caracola» (AP, 188) he sees himself as «una forma cautiva,» conditioned by his past («todo tu ayer») and trapped in his future both by necessity and finitude («todo tu porvenir, entre la arena»). Grounded like the conch, the poet reflects a despairing mood: «Y estás aquí, frente al hombre desnudo/ sin sol, bajo la luz de fuego,/ ni esperanza de huir, frente al abismo.»

It is enough for the poet to experience the contingency of the world and the tenuousness of his grasp of it for it to be called radically into question: «Pasa, como una brisa, el corazón del tiempo./ Anoche ya no es más que un recuerdo triste,/ un cerrar de la puerta/ para quedarnos herméticamente solos...» (DTA, 31). This sense of the transitoriness of life, the certainty that the real and the ideal will drift apart and be lost in the flux of things demands of the poet that he extract the most from each moment. Certainly, as a writer, the present acquires special urgency; ideas must be recorded straightaway and without hesitation:

> ... Y es que las horas y los días nos engañan,
> y nos dicen que hay tiempo, muchos años
> por delante, y nosotros creemos
> y esperamos. ...
> Pero no, hay que decirlo ahora,
> hay que cantar cuando aún hay canto
> y decírnoslo mientras que podemos...
> («Asonante final,» AP, 266)

The poet is often moved to stay the course of time by submerging himself in the present tense. Nowhere is the leap into immediacy more forcefully portrayed than in «Variación de un soneto» (AP,

90). Set in a menacing and nocturnal landscape, the mood created by the poem is one of inexorable dread and anxiety in the face of mutability. Striving to brush away the cobwebs of time and to enclose himself in the moment, the poet engages in frenzied celebration of a hoped-for renascence:

> . . . *Voy de nuevo a respirar con el aliento sin fronteras,*
> *sin recuerdos de ayer, sin hierro de torturas,*
> *hundidos al descenso de una luna caída sobre el mar.*
>
> *Rojo el labio por anhelo de ser vivo en el goce,*
> *fuera de los minutos que pasé en el vientre de la madrugada,*
> *iré a clavar mis dedos recién nacidos en el pecho de las*
> *azucenas.*

The poet is acutely conscious of being bound in a linear time that impedes him from partaking of the eternal flow and recurrence of nature. In «De la luz» (AP, 78), in a series of comparisons prefaced by the counterposition of «luz» with an admonitory «pero,» he exhorts man to confront the truth of his contingency:

> . . . *Luz, sí. Luz, hasta quebrarnos el alma al viento en mil*
> *gusanos de colores,*
> *pero con ese fijo pensamiento de que mañana entrará la luz*
> *sobre nosotros y ya no la veremos.*

The grim image of finitude expressed in the final verse («mañana estará la luz sobre nosotros y ya no la veremos») is later extrapolated and used independently in «Palabra poética» of *Poema Mío,* (AP, 225), whereby its force is magnified by reiteration and condensation.

The futility of man's hunger for permanence is underscored in the poem «Del dolor» (AP, 95). The relentless repetition of the word «dolor» in the introductory and final stanza, and the disquieting interrogatives of the middle stanza crest into a paroxysm of existential despair. Within genuine freedom of choice, failure, is, perforce, placed on the same footing as success:

> . . . *¿Y la libertad, y el cantar extasiado en la cumbre*
> *de las montañas abiertas a los cuatro puntos cardinales,*

a qué sima rodaron, deshecha la voz y cegada la lumbre
hasta hundirse en un seno frío de cristales? . . .

The poet is obliged, again an again, to face himself in his being-unto-death. That time is death's courier, is articulated with savage intensity in «Homenaje a Shakespeare» (DTA, 61):

. . . el miedo de soñar, de comer nuestro pan entre la angustia
de lo que nos rodea;
la muerte a la que nutren las semillas del tiempo;
el tiempo mismo, torpe lazarillo
que nos lleva inseguro por la escena
cual temeroso comediante nuevo;
el cuento de un idiota, que no nos dice nada . . .

Time as a «torpe lazarillo» may stumble and have accidents yet the denouement of life's meaningles tale, «el cuento de un idiota,» has already been prescribed. Only man, in his blindness (i.e., in need of a «lazarillo») is unable to forejudge the moment or place of this finale, hence «el miedo de soñar, de comer pan entre la angustia.»

The same anxious dread is evidenced in the powerful conclusion of the poem «El viajero» (DTA, 55) when, taking account of the failing light of dusk, the poet wonders what the morrow brings. The haunting final interrogation, «¿hasta mañana?» is an eloquent distillation of the poet's acutely sensed mortality.

These ideas are again amply developed in the the poem «Pasar» (AP, 355). Here, suggesting the futility of man's struggle against time, the poet appears to endorse a fatalistic surrender to life's journey-unto-death. («Hay que pasar, como los días,/ como las nubes por el cielo . . .»). In the first verse of stanza II, the repeated use of verbs of motion, the enjambement with the second verse, the emphasis on adverbs of time, suggest a relentless process which fuses the three *ec-stases* of time («Pasar, seguir pasando, yendo/ de ayer, por hoy, hasta maña-na»). Yet, verses three and four intimate a wavering resolve, greatly accentuated further on, in the face of death («Y tal vez desear descanso/ ya con las manos enlazadas»). The difficulty and cost of this journey into a future that is already prescribed are suggested syntactically and even phonetically in the first verse of stanza IV («Ir a mañana, por ir yendo/ por seguir, como sigue el agua»). Yet, man remains but a reluctant traveler, for in this process he is carried to an abyss of nothingness which swallows all meaning («Y temer que al pasar los días/ se nos ponga marchita el alma/ en la absoluta soledad/ cuando ya no nos quede nada»). Why man experiences his contingency agonically is revealed in the last stanza («No nos queda más que el sentir/ cómo todo se marcha huyendo/ y sólo vayan a quedarnos/ como clavos los pensamientos»): Unlike those elements of the natural universe cited in the poem («los días,» «las nubes,» «el agua») man alone is «nailed» by his thoughts to the crucifix of his finitude.

While the poem «Nocturno I» (AP, 110) shows that the whole world partakes of this process («. . . el mundo se perdió una vez, y otra , y otra/ y se estará perdiendo siempre, gracias al porvenir . . .»), only man in his conscious awareness stands as helpless witness of his own mortality.

The poet's view of reality, then, in the poems studied in this section, is that it is a show of accidental events of which only one thing can be said with certitude: it passes. Reality is essentially pastness; it is as desultory as it is fleeting.

Death as an Adversary

The poems under study here represent an externalization of sensible rather than intellectual responses to death. Viewed from the strict perspective of the «hunc et nunc,» death is seen as an adversary advancing on man's terrain and encroaching on his dreams of fulfillment («Tanto sueño y la muerte,» AP, 138), possessing, absorbing, destroying: «El sueño y la muerte están dentro de nosotros desde el principio. Primero el sueño puede más; llena los días despiertos y las noches dormidas. Luego la muerte se va entrando, nos va destruyendo, absorbiendo, poseyendo hasta el beso último, cuando se encuentra frente a nuestro sueño y lo vence.»(4) A similar sense of this implacable process is conveyed in the already cited poem, «Homenaje a Shakespeare.» Here, «blind» to man's anguish, death «grows» within man, «inundates» his being, and «carries» him to his appointed destiny. The final encounter with death, described elsewhere as a «blanca inquietud,» «este minuto negro y ahogado,» as a meeting up with «el filo de la muerte,»(5) is characterized here as a

40

«naufragio último.» Always, the disquieting attributes of death are emphasized in the poems under study here.

Occasionally, Florit succeeds in defusing and displacing his personal trepidation by differentiating between two types of death, a «bad death» seen in a larger socio-historic context, and a «good death» that one is prepared to receive. These distinctions, framed against the backdrop of war, are clearly posited in «Conversación a mi padre» (AP, 234) and in «Para empezar» (DTA, 23):

> . . . [Man] Lo que quiere es que siga
> esta danza tremenda de la muerte
> que no es la muerte tuya y mía
> --es decir, la de andar por casa,
> la que se recibe en zapatillas
> o cuando más en el campo abierto
> o en el agua limpia--
> sino la otra, la muerte a montones
> en los campos cerrados y las aguas pestíferas,
> la mala muerte que baja del aire
> y que sale de donde estaba escondida
> para aplastar los cuerpos como nueces
> y segar las cabezas como espigas . . .

In «Para empezar,» the poet takes measure of the year just past:

. . . Porque hay que ver que ha sido malo.
No lo digo por mí, gracias a Dios, sino para este mundo
que no sabe salir de tanto enredo y tanta muerte,
y tanto muerto que sin comerlo ni beberlo
se ha visto, y se verá, lejos, con una bala dentro.
Y al norte y al sur, al este y al oeste.   Todos matándose
porque sí, porque tú, porque yo, porque nosotros, vosotros.
Y todos caínes y todos malditos.   Todo el que mata, sí, maldito.
Como maldito sea el que manda matar.
Maldita sea y muera la muerte.
Quiero decir la que no llega como debe de ser, tranquila . . .

Again, in «La muerte en el sol» (AP, 222), the poet acknowledges the larger social ills that beset the world, and «el tiempo de horror, tiempo de muerte.» Yet, even when death is so depersonalized, it still strikes terror in the poet's heart: «Ese terror de recibir la muerte en un día de sol. . . .»

It is, therefore, with understandable loss of self-possession, encapsulated in the title of the poem «El miedo» (DTA, 25), that the poet stands before the fact of his own brief existence. Seen from the perspective of personalized fear, death becomes, in several poems, a menacing, lurking force which stalks its prey and from which the poet must hide:

> . . . *Y aquí dentro, un temor de ser visto por la muerte*
> *antes de ser un poco más . . .*
>
> («El miedo,» DTA, 25)
>
> . . . *La muerte escondida,*
> *acechando con ojos de espera . . .*
>
> («Del dolor,» AP, 95)
>
> *Borraré el grito sin palabras que me iba naciendo*
> *al sentirme, de un polo al otro de la noche,*
> *música al tropezar con la cara de muerto asomada a los*
> *cristales . . .*   («Variación de un soneto,» AP, 90)

The anxiety experienced here by Florit is of a visceral nature, uncurbed by laws of reason or faith. It is the poet in his material being that strains against the finality of death. The final verses of «Canción de la sombra» (AP, 69) admirably capture the truth of this struggle for containment and continuance, for a rootedness in time and space: «Para contener la vida/ el silencio de unos astros/ multiplicaba mis pies.» Christian resignation or stoic acceptance of death does not figure in these poems. In their bleak landscapes, God is curiously absent, for they have been wrought from the anguish of the poet's secular and temporal self. When God does appear, as in «Canción del final» (AP, 72), he is depicted as the creator of death, an impassive marksman grounding life with his arrow. While the point of view of the poet is not projected in this poem, the mood created by him is, nonetheless, one of desolation in which life ceases at the hands of a non-benevolent God.

> . . . *Suspenderán sus juegos los niños de todas las aceras*
> *y vendrá el viento para siempre a deshacer el goce develado,*
> *cuando todo esto que hoy alza el vuelo caiga herido*

por la flecha de Dios sobre las aguas infinitas.

Even poems in which the poet is sustained by his faith often betray some disquiet in the face of death. In «Asonante final» (AP, 266), for example, the depiction of a tranquil encounter with a paternal God in the life beyond is sharply offset by the disturbing interrogatives, «¿No es verdad que es eso lo que pasa? ¿que yo no lo estoy inventando?» In «Lo de siempre» (AP, 246) man's unquestioning assumptions about the universe and its creator are portrayed as inadequate. But, if man's «knowledge» is, in fact, without substance the reality of the God addressed in the final Stanza is also subtly placed in doubt: «Ya ves, Señor, qué pena/ la de saberlo todo sin saberlo,/ y más aún la pena de no verte,/ aunque sabemos que estás en el cielo.» In «Seguidilla» (AP, 281), one of Florit's most grim poems, no admission to a kingdom of heaven beyond is envisioned. In the poet's anxious imaginings, the gates remain firmly barred: «Cuando me acerque/ nadie abrirá la puerta/ para que entre.»

The suggestion of gradations of death in several poems equally shatters belief in an eternal life. Two levels of death are projected. The first involves admission to an antechamber of death built from the substance of memory, the «recuerdos» held by others that still endure. When these disappear, entrance is made into the dark emptiness of the final chamber of death. The poem «Conversación a mi padre» (AP, 234) finds the poet positioned at the first of these two levels. Here, carefully nurtured memories of his father promote the illusion of permanence thereby delaying passage way into that terrible, final chamber:

> *. . . es que, viviendo más, más te recuerda.*
> *Porque vive contigo, con lo que tú querías,*
> *con tus libros. (Aún tengo,*
> *en su cubierta gris, «Peñas arriba,»*
> *que te dejaste abierta*
> *aquel día . . .)*
> *Y seguimos viviendo todos*
> *y ya ves, recordándote todos los días.*
> *Y decimos: este postre le gustaba,*
> *y caminaba así, porque siempre iba aprisa,*
> *y una vez se afeitó el bigote*

> *y se lo volvió a dejar en seguida . . .*

However, in «Asonante final» (AP, 266), as already noted, both stages are delineated.   The progression from one to the other is clearly suggested in the poem's final passage:

> *. . . como se pierde todo lo que amamos,*
> *como me perderán los que me aman*
> *ese día, aquel día*
> *en que me quede sordo de verdad,*
> *sordo absoluto, ya definitivo,*
> *y me estén llamando,*
> *llamando,*
> *llamando*
> *por todas las esquinas de mi cuerpo,*
> *sobre todas las páginas de mis libros,*
> *entre toda las letras de mis versos,*
> *y no contestaré ¿qué habré de contestar?,*
> *porque ya de una vez y para siempre*
> *me habré quedado muerto.*

Here, in direct contrast to Dámaso Alonso's assertion that «se produce en el poeta el maravilloso salto desde la materia caduca de nuesra vida a la permanente del arte,»(6) man's artistic legacy, his bridge to eternity collapses under the force of death.

Nowhere is this trajectory of death made clearer than in the poem «Lo que queda» (DTA, 53).   The poet moves from material finitude («la tierra . . . que desintegra y pulveriza/ y verdaderamente mata») into the first chamber of death where his unicity is reaffirmed through those things that define him:

> *. . . No importa, porque quedan nuestros versos,*
> *nuestro amor a la luz que sigue ardiendo,*
> *al amor mismo, a lo que hemos tocado*
> *y besado y guardado en el bolsillo.*
> *Y en el cajón del escritorio.*
> *Y la hojita de yerba en aquel libro.*
> *Y todo, todo lo que fuimos,*
> *lo que hemos de seguir siendo . . .*

Yet, the final three verses arrest all optimism, propelling the poet to his irrevocable destiny:

> . . . *hasta que, un día, una vez, alguien pregunte:*
> *¿qué es esto?, ¿quién lo guardó?, ¿para qué?, ¿cuándo?*
> *y entonces ya de verdad habremos muerto.*

«Real» death, then, as seen in these poems, brings with it the erasure of all traces of man's earthly existence. Inextricably fettered to the order of time and in an adversary relationship with death, the poet cannot give himself apocalyptic surety of immortality. His questions remain unanswered, his anxieties unassuaged.

Death as a Way of Life

That death is a permanent «fact of life» is clearly expressed by Florit in «Homenaje a Shakespeare» (DTA, 61): «Entre cuna y sepulcro/ arrastrarse muriendo a cada hora,/ y saber que esta muerte la llevamos/ desde el nacer. . . .» Cognition of this truth, with the concomitant loss of self-possession, does not necessarily function negatively but may be instrumental in a salutory release of emotion. The poet's flesh-and-blood response, the candorous disclosure of feeling are a measure of mental health and self-knowledge and act to lighten his burden, freeing him to pursue his assigned path.

A second group of poems, with which we will be primarily concerned here, suggests another formulation of the concept of death-as-a-way-of-life. They begin with the poet's conceptualization of his essential aloneness though he stands midst his fellow man. It is a separateness so complete and terrifying as to suggest an irrevocable dissolution of all bonds with the world and other finite creatures in it. No longer the productive solitude of normal self-concern, the «suficiente compañera» (AP, 211), the «perfecta soledad» (AP, 190) of earlier poems, this aloneness goes beyond the mournful acceptance of «El hombre solo» (AP, 342) or the alienated solitude of «El caminante» (AP, 337) which is subject to dissipation «frente al regalo de unos ojos.» Rather, the poet experiences an estrangement that carries with it the finality of death; it is «la absoluta soledad/ cuando ya no nos queda nada . . .» (AP, 355). The poet alternately suffers rejection at the hands of a «mundo no suyo» (DTA, 49), a world in which he must sojourn as alien, or, in turn, he acts to reject that world himself. The first of these alternatives holds in «El amante» (DTA, 43) where the poet is the unwilling and disconsolate outcast: «Porque al fin se está solo./ Y solo como un hongo al borde del camino,/ que no se atreve a tomar nadie, no sea venenoso . . . .» Similarly, in «Los poetas solos de Manhattan» (AP, 312), he identifies himself with the nameless, forgotten masses: «Lo que desean es dormir y olvidarse de todo--,/ olvidarse de que nadie se acuerda de ello,/ de que están solos, terriblemente solos, entre la multitud. . . .» The key poem «El solitario (DTA, 410), depicts this separateness as a penetrating cold, unrelieved by any warmth of human affection: «En esta hora de marzo, casi de noche ya,/ el hombre solo siente un gran frío en el alma. . . .» The poet surrenders to the icy grip of this aloneness and consciously bars all hatchways to escape. The acute awareness of his ontological solitude («El saberse tan solo en este momento/ que es como si toda la soledad del mundo/ se le hubiera metido en las entrañas . . .»), is coupled with the struggle to deny the feelings generated by it. In a perilous process of interiorization and sublimation, these are willfully buried in the hope they will be «lost» in a subterranean, «shadowy» realm, ultimately disappearing from the poet's consciousness: «No duele más que dentro, tan dentro que parece/ que lo de dentro se ha perdido en la tiniebla. . . .» Herein does the poet move to a different kind of solitude--one in which he not only acts to reject the world without, but also the cluster of emotions that assail him from within. In complete withdrawal from immediacy, he engages in a side step by which he diverts himself from the path of life. He strives to abrogate the contradictory laws of life which beckon, tempt, and threaten, by living *aeterno modo* in a state of nonlife, in retreat from actions, consequences, regrets, and feelings. The peace described in the poem «La paz» (DTA, 33) clearly illustrates this retraction for it appears to be won at the expense of life itself and in abstraction from time:

> . . . *¿Desde cuánto tiempo*
> *esa paz, ese hablar, ese callarse*
> *en los dos pensamientos?*
> *Pero antes --yo lo sé-- hubo la angustia,*

el no saber la hora y el inquieto
mirar para el reloj.   Era la vida,
la otra, la de ayer, la falsa otra
que nos hiere de ardor, y no rechaza
y nos deja un poquito más pequeños . . .

By withdrawing from the arena of decision or action the poet can also deny time's flow. The poem «Canción del silencio» (AP, 73) describes such a stasis or suspension in time. Safe from the «inquietud de unas horas futuras,» the poet exults in the «perfect» stillness and silence which are coterminous with nonlife:

. . .Los segundos del sol bajaron a beber aguas muertas
donde nacía la inquietud de unas horas futuras
prontas a alzar el vuelo con las palomas de la tarde.
Aquel minuto se extendía sobre las ramas inmóviles,
abriendo una luz sin ecos, ni cantos, ni nada . . .

In the poem «La puerta» (AP, 330), withdrawal is again equated with paralysis. The climate of the poem is more personal as the poet, transfixed with dread before the symbolic door of the poem's title, is virtually held rooted in time and space: «Y los pasos, clavados en la sombra/ no eran más que silencio. . . .» Unable to bring himself to unravel the mystery of existence («Y, ¿cómo por el hombre solo/ desvanecer el hueco del silencio? . . .»), the poet opts for retreat and indefinite postponement: «Mejor así. Para llamar hay tiempo.»

That denial of life is the price of serenity is again expressed forcefully in the poem «La niebla» (AP, 356). The symbolic «mist» eclipses those aspects of reality that most perplex and bother: «Es mejor lo nublado/ Es mejor no ver nada claramente. . . .» A crescendo of meaning is plotted by virtue of the sixfold repetition, with some variation, of «Es mejor no ver» which reaches its climax in the paroxysmic final verse: «Mas, sobre todo, no ver, no mirar, estarse ciego/ y poder ser feliz entre la niebla.» Safely removed from the barbs of Eros, from time--the courier of Thanatos, from the joys, the sorrows, the rejections that form the very fiber of life, the peace encountered by the poet exists only in a sterile death-in-life.

Elsewhere, withdrawal expresses itself as steely indifference toward life which is «suffered» rather than lived («¿Qué llega un año más?   Pues a aguantarlo,» DTA, 33) or endured in the shattering silence of aloneness. In «Desde la nieve» (AP, 348) the elements of the poem are carefully selected and strung together so as to maximize the absence of redeeming life forces:

Desde la nieve convertida en agua,	(Diminished, dissolved, impure)
desde el sucio periódico sin dueño,	(Orphaned, sullied)
desde la niebla, desde el tren hundido	(The former obscures, separates; the latter is submerged and propelled on a subterranean, lightless course)
con sus cientos de manos que buscan asidero;	(Synecdoque which dramatizes a sense of imbalance, the need for something to «hold on to»)
desde la fantasía de los anuncios luminosos y el ruido sin piedad de bombas de incendio;	(The stridency of reality)
desde la noche que nos cae encima	(Night as an agressive, oppressive force)
--losa de cielo sin estrellas--;	(The celestial signs are not visible)

desde cada momento perdido	
entre las calles	
donde todos los solos del mundo	(Flickering identification
pasan desconocidos;	with others equally lost)

desde el árbol sin hojas y	(Empty of promise or life)
el camino sin gente,	

otra vez, como ayer, como	(Empty sameness of time, cur-
mañana	tailed by death alone)
acaso ya como todos los días	
que vendrán, si es que vienen,	

entro al silencio	(Brevity underscores the
	silence of a solitude equiva-
	lent to a state of nonlife)

In «Nadie conversa contigo» (AP, 351), the author is conscious of «el tiempo del reloj,» yet maintains his detachment from present and future tense. The «melancólico no» of his present is uncorrected and unmodified by the knowledge that «los otros viven aunque viven con dolor.» The tacit acknowledgment that he is living a death is apparent in the following verses:

> . . . *La sombra sube, sin miedo,*
> *de quien ya se la aprendío;*
> *de quien ajusta su vida*
> *a una terca negación,*
> *viendo cómo pasan nubes*
> *por un cielo sin color,*
> *viendo que los otros viven*
> *aunque viven con dolor;*
> *viendo ajenas soledades*
> *rotas de separación . . .*

«El olvidado» (DTA, 29) is one of the most disturbing of Florit's nihilistic poems for its dispassionate and numbed quietude. In focusing on his death-in-life, Florit creates a climate of stillness reminiscent of the poem «La paz.»

> . . . Algún día me siento vivo
> y otros, los más, como si muerto,
> con mucho aire para el alma
> y mucha tierra sobre el cuerpo;
> ya sin temores ni esperanzas
> para siempre callado y quieto . . .

The same nihilism is apparent in the poem significantly entitled «El casi muerto» (DTA, 31). Here the poet underlines the inadequacy of action, or language as agents of communication. Always, we are destined to remain «herméticamente solos» in a state parallel to death which, here, is experienced in degrees: «No se sabe qué muere si cerramos los ojos/ como si ya estuviéramos del todo muertos. . . .»

However, it is in the extraordinary poem «Para después» (DTA, 45) that the concept of death-in-life receives complete certification. Here, the transition from life to death is made «sin angustia» for a cessation of vital forces, a diminishment of faculties, an abstraction from time has already taken place; the protagonist finds that he is, in fact, already dead. While the poem is formulated anecdotally in the third person, the direct autobiographical allusions to Florit's love of painting, music, and poetry, and the final parenthetical reference to the ravages of Eros creates an intensely personal climate. This, in combination with masterful understatement and stylistic control makes «Para después» one of the most perfectly poised poems of Florit's opus:

> Ya no pudo pintar.   Estaba ciego.
> Las teclas del piano, la pluma, ya sin dedos.
> Como tenía los oídos sordos
> y ya estaba cansado de sus piernas,
> un día, allá en el tiempo
> --había sol, el aire estaba quieto--
> se dispuso a morir.
> Se tendió sin angustia sobre el suelo.
> Y cuando vino a ver, ya estaba muerto.

(Tenía, además, el corazón deshecho).

Of the various responses, then, to death-as-a-way-of-life of which the poet is capable, it is the alienation, the ontological solitude of the last poems that are the most disturbing. For, a carefuly study of Florit's poetry reveals that the greatest peril to the poet does not lie in excess of anxiety in the face of his mortality, but in nihilistic disengagement from the reality of his life.

An Iconography of Disquiet

Nature as Flux

Florit's poetic opus is based, in large measure, on devoted attention to the natural world. Inwardly attuned to nature's messages, Florit relates to it both passively and actively. Passively, he opens his heart to the impulses it transmits to him; actively, he projects his own imagination onto the natural world, half creating the values that he finds there. External nature is used to clarify and give body to inward feeling and, in turn, inward feeling gives significance to external nature. This dual approach to nature results in an interfusion of the low and high, the finite and infinite, matter and spirit. Always, the love of nature serves to sharpen the poet's vision and deepen his capacity to feel.(7)

The poetry of «outwardness» of *Trópico* and the special view of nature it imparts have already been considered. For the purpose of this chapter, it is Florit's active and subjective involvement with nature in a poetry of «inwardness» that is the most telling for, here, nature simply acts as an ideogram of the poet's emotions, character, and experience. Specifically, we are concerned with nature as objective correlative of the poet's disquiet in the face of instability, uncertainty, and impermanence. When framed in this perspective, it is temporal nature rather than an immutable realm that beckons the poet, commanding his attention. The passing flux of immediate things in a shifting phenomenal world confirms and heightens the apprehensions that haunt him.

The sense of fragmentation, the lack of repose, the invevitable decomposition of all material things are expressions of the changes and process in the concrete natural world which are correlative to human life. Natural objects in the poems under study offer an iconography of transitoriness or death. The sea and light are frequently used in both these ways. Other emblems of transitoriness are clouds, flowers, mist, smoke, the seasons, the shifting sands. Images of death in the poems studied here center on night (an absence of light; an absence of «sky»; shadows; failing light), butterflies, doves, and the earth.

The poet deals with his feelings of disquiet in two principal ways: by abstracting them to an impassive natural realm thereby reducing their sting; by expressing them outright through forceful nature imagery. In the first instance, the poet-spectator objectively observes and dispassionately records impermanence as it appears in nature; it provokes no special anguish or outcry. Yet, abstractions and distance from the moment do not uniformly insure concealment of emotion, for in Florit's verses nature is alive and sentient and therefore subject to the same longings of the poet. Beyond its efficacy as a poetic trope, the personification of nature is central to the identification of the poet in his verse.

A second group of poems makes similar use of nature to express unending flux but with one important difference: now, without evasions, the poet speaks directly from the heart, from the epicenter of his «yo.» The point of view changes abruptly therefore, from that of nonintrusive author to poet-protagonist who formulates and articulates concerns and questions once abstracted or arcane. Because he connects squarely with himself, Florit is able, at these moments, to produce poems of special power and authenticity where the use of nature as symbolic representation of personal feeling is patently clear. It is *his* life that wanes like the «light» (AP, 50, 53, 55), *his* passing that carries him like the «stream» (AP, 355) to the final «sea» of death, *his* fear of the «abyss» (AP, 95), the «night» (AP, 90) of death and of the trampling of life's «flower» (AP, 128), *his* longing to reinsert himself in the «dawn» (AP, 90) of day that reverberate in these poems.

With these differences in perspective and focus delineated and understood, a closer look can be had at specific nature imagery.

The disorder and chaos of the universe described in the poem

«Homenaje a Goethe» (AP, 100) reveal with compelling force that it is the way of nature to be in constant flux, to be combining into ever more complex molecules, cells, organs, and organisms, and to be separating and breaking up only to recombine in other shifting wholes. Depicting the universe in its cosmogonic beginnings, the poet takes in the geological and astronomical mutations, and the large scale transformation of a primordial world. Through personification, inchoate elements of the universe--bodies of water, land, fire, celestial bodies--experience anxiety amidst primary chaos, and are desirous of boundaries and definition. Their apprehension, conveyed metaphorically and by personification, are described as «pensamientos ígneos,» «largo sufrir de las entrañas de la tierra indecisa,» «el miedo de correr desprendida,» «el inquieto palpitar,» «tanto bullir de formas sin destino seguro,» and «agudas interrogaciones.» The desire for definition and containment of these elements reflect man's longings, *ab aeterno,* for a tidy universe, a universe shaped by his ordering intelligence in despite of nature. Once again, the powerful use of nature serves as a speculum of the poet's obsession with flux.

Light, a foremost symbol of the poems under study in this chapter, stands as an analogue of mortal life: its intensity, its brightness, and duration, thus, are vital indices of resilience or slack. Conversely, its absence can be taken as an analogue of death, with transitoriness as its immediate corollary. While these are clearly interrelated, it is useful to consider them separately.

In «Canción para leer» (AP, 67), while the fragmentation and diminishment of light are described, there is no attempt to derive from this any implications for humanity. As an element of nature, light is made to suffer and endure impermanence with no accent on renewal. Taking note of the flickerings, gleamings, and dartings that prelude final fragmentation, emphasis is placed, as follows on «la esencia luminosa caída en rayos por el mundo,» «la evasión definitiva,» «el color partido,» «la unidad deshilvanada.» This is capped by a final comparison and personification: «Hay que saber el dolor de verse triturado en el yunque/ para comprender cómo llora la luz el vuelo de sus almas.» Equally, swift changes of light and loss of unity are noted and recorded in the following verses:

Brillan luces voladoras
tan sueltas sobre la casa,
como luminosa masa
partida en tenues auroras.
Entre las brisas sonoras
son átomos de diamante . . .(AP, 50)

Como al cristal llegan las luces
de los minutos pasajeros . . .(AP, 64)

. . . quiébrase el sol en cristales
al caer en desiguales luces . . . (AP, 47)

. . . esta luz que ahora viaja de prisa en el aire
ya no tendrá vivas las alas . . . (AP, 72)

. . . Y hecha de trémolos inciertos,
de toda aquella luz quebrada . . . (AP, 327)

Elsewhere, light imagery is employed in association with the fragility of the human condition, for man's dreams, glories, and possessions share closely in the fleeting quality of light as the following examples reveal: The dissipation of man's triumphs and glory linked with light in indirect association («Soledades/ de luz en torno cambian trayectorias/ y ya recuerdo son todas las glorias/ que un instante volaron a su cumbre,» AP, 87); man's existential freedom, his exultant hymn to life («¿Y la libertad, el cantar extasiado en la cumbre/ de las montañas abiertas a los cuatro puntos cardinales/ a qué sima rodaron, deshecha la voz y cegada la lumbre,» AP, 95); temporality and loss as man's manifest destiny («Ay, qué destino triste el de tantos arroyos sin ventura;/ cómo se va dejando atrás el eco rubio de las primaveras;/ y qué dolor de noches apagadas/ éste de sentir que las cosas van hundiéndose con el ocaso de/ los días,» AP, 110. «. . . Viene a pasar como nosotros/ como la luz de nuestro otoño . . .» AP, 325).

In the poems «En el tren» (AP, 323) and «El viajero» (DTA, 55), the duration of light as an index of man's allotted time is faced intrepidly and with panic respectively. In the first, the repetition of the adverbs «todavía» and «aún» (four times and two) in reference to light, serves to stretch the day in an effort at prolongation. Pureness of color (rojo vivo, verde, cielo azul) suggests a vitality as yet undiminished. In conjunction with a light that *is* «todavía,» the poet surveys the natural scene with composure: «Y todavía,/ el pensamiento alegre/ que de dentro nos mira. . . .» The reader foresees that the erasure of one «todavía» (the light) is conjoined to the erasure of the other (the poet's serenity).

In «El viajero,» the poet cognizes his immediate link with the impermanence of light, and awaits the falling of dusk with trepidation:

> . . . *Como no es juego este momento*
> *de soledad junto a la tarde--*
> *Viendo que la luz se va marchando*
> *y morirá dentro de un rato ¿ hasta mañana?*

A metaphorical distinction is made, in several poems, between the quality of light of the divergent seasons. The aging poet shrinks, for example, from the luminosity of spring, the long stretch of day that illumes the empty darkness of his life. Psychologically, he seeks the gray penumbra of winter whose brief days and long nights stand as an ideogram of his existence. Yet, even winter's frail light is, at times, an unwelcome intrusion on the poet's solitude: «Afuera, el sol/ con frío de invierno/ ilumina mi afán . . .» (AP, 349).

Equally, an absence of light may signify a death-in-life («mis días sin luz» [AP, 347], «toda la luz perdida» [AP, 125]), as the poet moves along a path of «ocasos tristes» (AP, 130). Still, despite his withdrawal from life's arena, the poet dreads the inexorability of time symbolized by a light which defines the boundaries of each new day: «Sólo el hombre infeliz se queja y sufre/ por la luz que se marcha, y por la aurora./ Por saberse sin sol en Primavera» (DTA, 50).

A connection between the cessation of light and death understood in a literal sense is also made forcefully by Florit in various poems as in «Canción del final» (AP, 72). At the very outset, the final quiescence of light impulses is directly yoked to death: «. . . toda esta luz que ahora viaja de prisa en el aire/ ya no tendrá vivas las alas y dormirá suspensa y fría. . . .» Again, in «Nocturno III» (AP, 116), the second of two oxymorons makes this relationship clear: «. . . con este sordo ruido de soles apagados. . . .»

The poem «Tarde presente» (AP, 171), which by its very title implies the push and pull of competing notions of time suggests that the poet's longing to partake of life is bound and constrained both by the contours of his «yo» and the reality of his finitude, again expressed by light imagery: «Entre el ocaso y yo, toda la vida. . . .» The desire for a miraculous continuance, a staying of life's course, is only possible within a nature gone askew. The poet's conjectures of freakish triumph over a natural order are again light-related: «Como si todo junto de repente/ se pusiera entre el hombre y su destino./ Como si ante el ocaso rojo abriera/ un girasol sus rayos amarillos. . . .» Yet, if in his fervent imaginings the poet eloquently portrays man (el girasol) in triumph over time (el ocaso), these illusions of endurance are short-lived. Indeed, and by antiphrasis, the poems «Otoño» (AP, 262), «El otro ardor» (AP, 264), and «El hombre solo» (AP, 342) suggest an implacable waning of light, a darkening of life's horizons tied to seasonal changes withing a normalized natural order:

> . . . No.   Ya la tierra aguarda
> que llegues tú, que vuelvas
> a cerrarle los soles . . .

(«Otoño»)

> . . . Como cruje al morir la enredadera
> por los vientos de otoño sola y seca
> junto al morir del sol que brilla apenas . . .

(«El otro ardor»)

> . . . triste de soledad cuando anochece. . . .
> Que el aire del invierno me rodea
> para purificarme de mis sueños
> y así dejarme a lo que soy: un hombre
> solo y, por desvalido, un alma seca
> al amor de la lumbre que se apaga . . .

(«El hombre solo»)

the absence of light as a signifier of death is chillingly conveyed in the poem «La puerta» (AP, 330). The door as final passageway through which all are destined to cross embodies, through personification (verses two and three), the very qualities associated with the dark nothingness of death which lies beyond (verse four):

> *Había que llamar.   Pero la puerta*
> *en lo oscuro callaba*
> *como una muerte en pie.*
> *Detrás, ni luz ni ruido . . .*

Finally, in «Lo que queda» (DTA, 53), Florit eschews the use of metaphor in favor of a succinct definition of death whose primary significance for the poet, once again, is the irrevocable loss to him of light:

> *Aunque después la tierra nos proteja*
> *hasta de todo, menos de su abrazo*
> *que desintegra y pulveriza*
> *y verdaderamente mata.*
> *Aunque un día la luz se nos nubló*
> *para siempre [la de aquí abajo, digo] . . .*

In Florit's poetry, then, chiaroscuro images are clearly interchangeable as poetic signs and, at times, join forces as double-barreled emblems of time:

> *. . .Ay, qué destino triste el de tantos arroyos sin ventura;*
> *cómo se va dejando atrás el eco rubio de las primaveras;*
> *y qué dolor de noches apagadas*
> *éste de sentir que las cosas van hundiéndose con el ocaso de*
> *los días. . .* (AP, 110)

A deliberate imbalance is provoked in these verses by offsetting a single reference to «el eco rubio de las primaveras» with the compound impact of «noches apagadas» and «ocaso de los días» which connote the irrevocable and overpowering force of death.

Movement toward death-within-life is again expressed in nocturnal images in the following excerpt with the «mist» of the second verse acting as signifier of the darkness of night:

> *Este sentir que la vida se acaba*
> *y ya no ver más que niebla en redor. . . .*

> *Por el correr de la vida que acaba*
> *se entra a mirar cómo viene el morir,*
> *y ya vivir es un sueño sin forma,*
> *lejos del ser, en la noche sin fin . . .*(AP, 96)

Just as the shadows of night float irrevocably toward nothingness («. . . esta sorda angustia de mirarte la sombra/ que va por las tardes con el sol a la muerte,» AP, 191) so does the poet move on his assigned path to an encounter with his own death, enacted during a night of «forgotten dawn»: «Porqué tú eres más firme, oh mi noche de amaneceres/ olvidados./ Más que la luz por el destino condenada a beberse mis/ últimos adioses . . .» (AP, 119). The descriptive and limiting adjectives employed to describe night («firme,» «mi noche») suggest an equanimity that is, at best, illusory for elsewhere, the nocturnal drama of death inspires horror and despair.

The duration and quality of light is contingent on both chronological and seasonal variables. Once a celebrant of light, the elderly poet cannot abide the luminosity of spring whose merciless glare only highlights the torment, the uncertainty, the anxiety of age: «. . . esa luz de afuera, de ese mundo no suyo,/ ¿qué ha de traer sino la incertidumbre? . . .» (DTA, 50). Painfully aware of his own decline, the poet knows himself to be «sin sol en Primavera.»

The winter of life fuses metaphorically with a winter of death in «La nieve» (AP, 135) where the properties of snow, its chill and lack of color prevail in all seasons: «. . . Pero no la tendrás (la nieve) eternamente/ como yo, blanca y fría/ bajo el cielo feliz de los veranos.» A similar linkage is made in «Pude escribir» (AP, 346): «. . . Ya es tarde para todo. Ya quisiera/ que este frío de enero, el viento helado/ se llevara con ellos lo que queda. . . .»

Autumn is personified as harbinger of death and sterility in «Otoño» (AP, 262). Despite a semblance of abstraction, the urgency of diction and lexicon, and the momentum generated by the verbs, suggest the poet is personally caught up in his theme:

> *No. Ya la tierra aguarda*
> *que llegues tú, que vuelvas*
> *a cerrarle los soles.*
> *A callarle los pájaros.*

A dejarle los árboles en seco,
así como quedan
en el medio del alma los recuerdos.
Secos --y alzados
sobre el fondo sin luz del cielo.
Que llegues a cortarle la sonrisa
de los últimos crisantemos,
y la llama volante de las hojas
entre su incendio.
Que le ciegues el agua
con la nieve.
Que le asordes el trino
con los vientos.
Y que, por Dios, al empezar noviembre
la dejes todo un día con sus muertos.

In Florit's iconography of flux, flowers remain the archtypal symbol of ephemeral beauty conveying, at once, a sense of permanence and of mutability. These opposing traits receive an equal accent in «Rosa» (AP, 283), «La rosa» (AP, 329), and «Seguro amor» (AP, 336). The first of these poems, while noting the fragility of the rose, counterposes this awareness of its fleeting form with a celebration of its permanent essence: «. . . tú, pura flor de ilimitada esencia/ llenas sobre tu cálida presencia/ un minuto de ardor entre la vida. . . .» Similarly, in «La rosa,» perishability is balanced by renascence in an endless, cyclic process which is posited in the poem: birth (rebirth): «Nueva-mente, la rosa . . . De nuevo se alza . . . nueva siempre»; pleni-tud and decline: «. . . Allí, en su centro, con la carne/ pálida y retorcida de los pétalos,/ la rosa vive aún, por el ocaso/ cada vez más sin luz, más detenido»; death: «Y en él, segura de la muerte, espera/ viento o mano fatal que se la lleve/ al reino del no ser, por haber sido.» The counterpositioning of the fleeting and the enduring atributes of flowers is again evident in «Seguro amor»: «Besar la flor . . . Es confesar amor por lo que dura/ y por lo que después irá pasando . . . El labio que besó la flor sabía/ unir la eternidad con el ocaso.»

At other moments, the poet is less evenhanded, and chooses to stress transitoriness at the expense of renewal as in «Otra canción para leer» (AP, 70). While the life cycle of the flower, posited in the third stanza, seems to intertwine the three strands of time («. . . sabe que desde ayer que irá mañana . . .») it closes on a final note of «angustia» with no promise, as elsewhere, of renascence:

> Todo está ya en esta semilla que aguarda entre la tierra
> el día de asomarse al espectáculo del mundo con una flor en
>   la sonrisa.
> Ya sabe desde ayer que irá mañana a estarse quieta entre
>   unos dedos
> en los que sólo queda un anillo y el ademán lleno de
>   angustia.

Again, in «Canción de seis pétalos» (AP, 63) the accent is on perishability as the poet records, with impassive mien, a flower's final hour.   Chiaroscuro effects are in evidence:

> Vive lejana de su piedra
> con la parábola vencida;
> fija al extremo de su vida
> por el dolor de su hora negra.
> Punto de luz, a la salida
> de tanta sombra que la arredra,
> juega a morir entre los brazos
> de sus innúmeros pedazos.

Yet, in «Canción para leer» (AP, 67), the desperate flight of the «claveles despedazados» is softened by the vision of a celestial realm where a reflowering is, in fact, possible:

> …Ya se irán esparciendo como semillas en el volar sin norte
> para los múltiples surcos hendidos en el cielo.
> Ya tendrán dosel y cuna entre cristales y sobre los élitros
>   tendidos,
> encima de la gota de agua y de los ojos deslumbrados.

The butterfly, too, is found to be a symbol, par excellence, of transitoriness in Florit's poems.   In «Soneto,» #2 (AP, 85), it is described as «tormented» and, in the absence of permanence and certitude, is engaged in «agitated flight.»   Again, in «A la mariposa muerta» (AP, 133), the butterfly shares both in man's «jubilation» and in his «disquiet» signifying with its death man's «lost illusions» and his «despairing thoughts.» Butterflies in flight connote death in «Canción para leer» (AP, 67) while their disorientation in «Canción del final» («. . . ya no sabrán qué rumbo han de tomar las mariposas,» AP, 72) conveys a sense of apocalyptic disorder and panic.

A release from life is linked to the tremulous flight of doves in various poems suggesting the soul's pathway as it soars to celestial heights. In «Para tu ausencia» (AP, 98), the poet's father is guided on his final journey by «. . . un bando de palomas prendido a tus ensueños. . . .» Elsewhere, the presence of doves is an augur of death's imminence: «Este sentir que la vida se acaba . . . Tibio rozar de palomas en vuelo . . .» (AP, 96). «. . . Ya se me acerca el filo de tus puñales;/ ya para abrirme el alma cómo te asomas/ en ese vuelo trémulo de palomas/ a beber la amargura de mis cristales» (AP, 118).

In various poems, the earth parallels the poet's vulnerability to death. This identification is unmistakable in «El miedo» (DTA, 25) where the writer's defenselessness in the face of death is compared to the earth's «herida abierta en el centro del suelo . . .» a forceful image of gaping openness. Yet, in his poem «Lo que queda» (DTA, 53), the earth turns on the poet and is presented as a savage adversary. As if in premonition of the cyclic movement from «dust to dust,» Florit shrinks from the earth's embrace which «really» kills: «Aunque después la tierra nos proteja/ hasta de todo, menos de su abrazo/ que desintegra y pulveriza/ y verdaderamente mata. . . .»

The most doleful dwelling on man's finitude is encountered in the poem appropriately entitled «Del dolor» (AP, 95). Here, the rapid dispersal of smoke acts as a symbolizandum to smoke as a symbol of flux: «Dolor, dolor, dolor. Más que el dolor de la vida/ para esta ráfaga de humo tendido a los vientos. . . .» The poem's final verse, which identifies smoke with man's thought («la ráfaga de humo de mi pensamiento») clarifies the poet's intent and heightens the tone of existential anguish, for death carries not only the corporal nullification of man, but erases the realm of his ideas as well. Nature imagery again forcefully suggests that man's struggle for immortality is futile.

The sea.--In Florit's poetry, the sea is tied to the realm of birth and death, generation and flux. Understandably, then, the feelings the sea inspires within the poet are often complex and contradictory, depending on which facet is stressed, and can veer from dread to desire, disquiet to serenity. Differing responses mirroring variability of mood customarily are encompassed within discrete poems. However, a double view of the sea is at times projected within the corpus of a given poem. In «El mascarón de proa» (AP, 248), for example, the many historic and geographic variables of the bodies of water described are offset and even subsumed by the sea taken as a quasi-Platonic form which remains unchanged: «. . . Y qué abrazos tú a mí, mi mar constante. . . .» Similarly in «Atlántico» (AP, 59), the lower recesses of the sea are fecund with new life («. . . subían las flores marinas a prenderse a su pecho./ Tanto germen de madera, y botones de nácar y cráneos/ florecidos en árboles verdes con frutas de un oro olvidado . . .») yet, contemporaneously suggest a menacing, infernal sphere, e.g. the persistent allusion to a «continente perdido,» to a wave «que cubría infiernos con su sonrisa interminable.» Again, in the first *décima* of «Mar» (AP, 51) the sea, apostrophized here by the poet, carries within it both the flowering of new life and the chill of death: «. . . como ya dentro floreces/ en escamas . . . El alma tuya --tan fría-- no más, por el beso, muerta. . . .»

At times, the push and pull of ambiguous feelings toward the sea are so marked as to express themselves within a single verse: «Agua errante y fija . . . (AP, 101) Mar cambiante y fijo . . . (AP, 226) Porque el destino tuyo mar, de muerte y de vida . . . (AP, 190) quedan las olas/ en su inquietud de agua serena . . . (DTA, 35) Llanto risueño y el llanto medroso de las lejanías/ navegaban en las frías rutas . . . (AP, 55).

When seen through the prism of mutability and flux, the sea enacts a natural law of change, fragmented and replenished, dispersing and regathering in other temporary and shifting wholes: «. . . ¿Qué sabe el mar de sus pedazos/ metidos en la tierra? . . . ¿Será cierto que no conserva nada? . . .» (AP, 75). Man's transitoriness is linked to that of the sea in «La pasajera» (AP, 325): «. . . Viene a pasar como nosotros . . . Viene a correr con el ruido/ de estar cumpliendo su destino. . . .» In the same poem, the verbs «pasar,» «correr,» «sonar,» «pulir,» «lamer,» «remolinear,» «saltar,» «reír,» «pasar,» «morir» are vehicles which reverberate allegorically, depicting life's way. The compression of the birth-death cycle in twenty-two verses emphasizes the constant motion of water as a symbol of time's unresting force. In «Tiempo» (AP, 328), the inalterable process of rise and fall, begun when «. . . la hora se le llena/ de tiempo y de canción,» spills out into a final sea «Que va a dar a lo que antes daba/ --tiempo y canción-- y va a caer/ como el tic-tac de una sonora arena/ en la orilla del mar aquel. . . .»

In numerous poems, the sea serves as an icon of finitude. Thus, in the twelfth *décima* of «Mar» (AP, 55) the «Náufrago suspiro,» the «total quebranto,» the «llanto risueño y el llanto/ medroso de lejanías,» projections of personalized feelings, are carried off on «ondas ya lejos,» reflected in the sea's «múltiples tenues espejos,» rushed along the water's pathways, «las frías rutas,» capped off by anguished awareness of time's flight, «la fuga de mis días.»

> *Náufrago suspiro tanto*
> *íbase en ondas ya lejos:*
> *múltiples tenues espejos*
> *para mi total quebranto.*
> *Llanto risueño y el llanto*
> *medroso de lejanías,*
> *navegaban en las frías*
> *rutas, a quedar ausentes*
> *de mí, por alados puentes,*
> *en la fuga de mis días.*

Haunted by the instability, the uncertainty, and constant change, the poet longs for a different reality. In «Soneto,» #3 (AP, 86), through personification, psychological projection, and transposition, the sea again is made to give expression to the poet's yearnings, hence the longing to remain fixed, stable, to come to final rest:

> *Quisieras, mar, desenvolverte en hojas*
> *--reiterada ilusión de verte quieto--,*
> *como si te sintieras más sujeto*
> *a cada impulso en que la tierra mojas.*
>
> *Por mucho que en espuma te deshojas*
> *vuelves atrás con tu caudal completo.*
> *(Caracol que retuvo tu secreto*
> *sólo guardó la voz con que te enojas.)*
>
> *Vaivén desolador del beso amante.*

Todo tu anhelo de morir diamante
que --orla la luz-- prendiérase a la arena,

queda preso, al final de la batalla,
en una voz, mientras la tarde calla,
resignada y pueril, vieja y serena.

Destined to a life-death cycle in perpetuity, the sea of the sixth *décima* of «Mar» (AP, 53) longs, in vain, for death as as resolution of flux:

Suspiro de opuesta vida
llega por camino ignoto
ya con el anhelo roto
y la esperanza partida.
¡Si arena clara, encendida
fuese tumba!   Ya lamento,
clama fracasado intento
de término.   Su desvío
rechaza despojo frío
vuelto en ondas por el viento.

Water as a destructive force has biblical roots.   *Ab initio,* primordial chaos was understood largely as an aquatic element for during Genesis «the spirit of God moved over the waters.» Florit's poem «Homenaje a Goethe» (AP, 100) forcefully depicts the chaotic rush of waters at the moment of cosmogonic beginning: «. . . Mar sin historia, con el balbuceo de sus aguas inquietas,/ caído de pronto en órbitas de un mundo ya vacías para siempre. . . .»   Several poems suggest that man is destined to move toward a final aquatic chaos as well.   Death as an «inquieto cántico de mares sin orillas» in «Nocturno III,» #5 (AP, 116) echoes the «canto sordo del mar sin fronteras» of primordial chaos in«Homenaje a Goethe.»   And, as in Genesis, God's presence is felt to hover over the waters in the apocalyptic moment as described in «Canción del final» (AP, 72).   After detailing the cessation of life elements, the poet shows how and when this will come to pass in the final two verses of the poem: «. . . cuando todo esto que hoy alza el vuelo caiga herido/ por la flecha de Dios sobre las aguas infinitas.»

The close association in which water and death are held is

palpably evident in other poems as well. The process of disengagement from this world and preparation for the next, for example, is transmitted in nautical and marine images in «Canción del nocturno» (AP, 66):

> Navego por las horas
> que más sufren el frío
> de un paisaje vivido
> más allá de estas cosas . . .
> Qué ríos me atraviesan
> de frías aguas tímidas . . .

When the view of the sea as death is in ascendancy, Florit shrinks from communion with its mysterious depths, for in his phantasmagoric vision, it is a fear-inspiring realm which stirs with secret life and with certain death. At these times, the poet prefers to fix his glance on the surface waters which, prism-like, catch and refract the sun's rays or serenely mirror a heaven «caído en regular geometría» (AP, 51).

Yet, often the dual pull of the sea which attracts and repels at once, impels the poet to further inquisitions. However, his probing glance on these occasions is «tense» thereby testifying to his disquiet:

> Puse la mirada tensa
> más que sobre ti, tan honda
> --desprecio para la onda
> y atención para la intensa
> vida que en tu seno piensa . . .(AP, 51)

Again, in the premonitory verse of «Canción de agua y viento» (AP, 75) the poet recoils from the sea's depths, twice urging flight («será mejor») from its lethal essences and decay:

> . . .Será mejor que el viento corra
> después de verse en un espejo de agua
> donde hay un fondo espeso de pétalos podridos.
> Siempre será mejor irse en el viaje de un minuto
> para olvidar que el veneno es azul . . .

Elements of nature repeatedly meet their death at sea in Florit's poems or, by virtue of personification, are made to sense with disquiet, that death is proximate. Rays of light, submerged and lost in the sea's depths in «Mar,» #4 (AP, 52), and transmuted poetically into «birds of light» display the same prescience of death:

> . . . *aves de tu luz, inquietas*
> *por un juego de saetas*
> *ilusionadas de cielo,*
> *profundas en el desvelo*
> *de llevar muertes secretas* . . .

Again, in «Mar» #5 (AP, 52), the sea is the final destination for a cloud which moves suicidally and, in chiaroscuro fashion, from a lightning streaked sky to its somber recesses:

> *Roto en espinas al peso,*
> *cielo, de urgente llamada;*
> *por anhelo de ser nada*
> *en marina cárcel preso,*
> *ábrese suicida beso*
> *de nube en sendas oscuras...*

The sea as a metaphor of death is equally apparent in other poems: «Fuego íntimo de todos los claveles despedazados/ corriendo a un mar sin forma, sin eco, sólo palabra . . .» (AP, 67). «. . . Me dirás tu color . . . y tu acento callado por el aire/ cuando caen al mar lo fríos ataúdes de tus muertos . . .» (AP, 117). «Qué ausencia, ya sin término,/ por nuevos oceanos . . .» (AP, 105). «. . . Te fuiste aquel minuto para toda la muerte/ a navegar en hondos oceanos de silencio . . .» (AP, 98).

However, it is in the poem «El miedo» (DTA, 25) that Florit's black vision of the sea as death is stated most explicitly and is directly linked to an awareness of his own finitude: «. . . Y aquí dentro, un temor de ser visto por la muerte/ antes de ser un poco más; antes de aquello/ que me espera: el mar. . . .»

The poems that have been studied in this section show that nature, whether portrayed as man's ally in his transient journey or as an agent of death, provides an iconography of flux and finitude and objectifies the disquiet this knowledge inspires.

Nature and Human Nature:
The Poet in Disharmony

Nature imagery has also been employed effectively to express other emotions that provoke disharmony in the poet. From Florit's presentation of these emotions there flows a double view of man's relationship to nature: one that suggests a bond between a sentient nature and the poet's deepest emotions as a unique individual; another that suggests a gulf between human nature and the rest of nature.

In the first instance, an empathic nature acts as a repository of the poet's feelings. Generally, Florit starts with a nexus of feelings and then imagines an appropriate natural setting that is correlative to them. For the most part feelings center on solitude, existential anguish, and love.

As a solitary wanderer, Florit may stand in isolation and estrangement from man but he remains linked to a nature which suffers equal impairment, hurt, or diminishment:

> *¿Dónde vas con la luz marchita?*
> *¿Dónde vas con el cielo roto?*
> *¿Dónde vas con el ala trunca?*

> *--Voy a estar con mi sueño solo.* (AP, 187)

In seeking to describe the sorrow that he feels, the poet repeatedly reaches for examples within a natural sphere as in «Canciones para la soledad,» #8 (AP, 182):

> *Tú no sabes, no sabes*
> *cómo duele mirarla.*
> *Es un dolor pequeño*
> *de caricias de plata.*

> *Un dolor como un árbol*
> *seco por la mañana.*

> *Un dolor sin orilla*
> *para dormir el agua.*

67

> *Un dolor como el rastro*
> *de la nube que pasa.*
>
> *Tú no sabes, no sabes*
> *cómo duele mirarla.*

Again, in the poem «En Bay Front Park» (AP, 285) Florit's «dolor presente» is equated to images of death, truncation, or ugliness in nature:

> *Aquí ya es otra cosa.*
> *Ese vaho de muerte cotidiana,*
> *ese viento de rota mariposa,*
>
> *quedaron a mis pies, ya desprendidos*
> *de polvo, de fango, y de veneno . . .*

Personal upheaval or solitude finds its match in nature:

> *Para ti la canción, águila herida,*
> *cisne de los crepúsculos sangrientos,*
> *pétalo de la flor estremecida*
> *por el abrazo de los vientos*
>
> *Para ti, cielo gris de la mañana*
> *vacía de la alondra y la amapola,*
> *y para ti, noche de voz lejana,*
> *de corazón sin fe, del alma sola . . .* (AP, 134)

The poet's solitary spirit fuses with a nature notably absent of life:

> *Está en el viento, pero no se mueve;*
> *en la flor, sin perfume;*
> *en el agua, sin onda; en el ocaso,*
> *sin fulgor; en el árbol, sin latido.*
>
> *Y está, sin alma ya, dentro del alma.* (AP, 184)

Again, in «Canción» (AP, 282), it is a frozen, forgotten moon that objectifies the poet's solitude:

> *. . . Ya tenía el yelo dentro*
> *cuando se cayó;*
> *ya tenía el yelo dentro,*
> *como yo.*
>
> *Toda la noche llorando*
> *para dormir;*
> *toda la noche llorando*
> *y no poderlo decir.*
>
> *Como estaba en el olvido*
> *se marchitó;*
> *como estaba en el olvido,*
> *como estoy yo . . .*

The surrender to feeling is at a high pitch in «Seguidilla» (AP, 281) and is again expressed through nature. Embarked on the lonely «path» of life, Florit here is engulfed metaphorically by the mist and cold of «night»: «Para llegar me falta/ mucho camino./ Toda la noche solo/ Con niebla y frío. . . .»

The collaborative bond between nature and human nature is again visible when muted sorrow is converted into existential despair. Man's «angst» in the face of nothingness is matched by diminishment and mortality in nature as in «Del dolor» (AP, 95). Here, like the «abismo de todas las hojas» and the «ráfaga de humo tendido a los vientos,» all traces of man's existence disappear from the face of the earth. Again, in «Homenaje a Goethe» (AP, 100), natural forces outside of man which move without measure or direction («vértigo de estar ya para siempre rodando ciega . . . formas sin destino seguro . . . pleamar de agudas interrogaciones») reflect the upheaval, the chaos of «maybes» that pulsate in man's inner life.

As documented under Eros, in Florit's poetry, sorrow in love finds an especially responsive echo in nature as in «Nocturno II» (AP, 112) where the poet's terrifying aloneness is reflected in the bleakness of nature. In «Preludio» (AP, 206), though passion is calmed by time's passage («en la resaca de mis años») the poet moves metaphorically from «afternoon» to «night» beneath the «cielo de mis nieblas» and in other verses the romantic correlation between the writer and nature is also palpably evident: «. . . El mundo y yo, cansados de esperar,/ quedamos solos, desvalidos, bajo la mirada de la estrellas/ muertas» (AP, 347). Nature, viewed from the perspective of lack or want acts as analogue to his own incompletion: «. . . desde la noche que nos cae encima/ --losa de cielo sin estrellas--; . . . desde el árbol sin hojas y el camino sin gente . . .» (AP, 348). «. . . viendo cómo pasan nubes/ por un cielo sin color» (AP, 351). The poet communes with a shadowy realm of endless night and muted voices:

Solo, lejos de ti, que ya no me escuchas
ni podrás escucharme ya más.
Hundido en mares de silencio
cuando la luz se aleja por el oeste
y las sombras se alargan como las alas de los grandes pájaros . . .
¿Qué esperar sino más soledades,
más días sin luz, más noches deshabitadas
de la hermosa caricia del sueño? . . . (AP, 347)

The arrid terrain of his soul is mirrored in a natural realm which bespeaks endings rather than beginnings: «. . . Cae el otoño con sus tristes hojas/ que giran a la luz de la ventana/ y al llegar, de cansadas, a la tierra,/ se deshacen al paso de las aguas . . .» (AP, 350). «. . . Ya es tarde para todo. Ya quisiera/ que este frío de enero, el viento helado,/ se llevaran con ellos lo que queda . . .» (AP, 346).

Clearly, then, in these poems, nature and human nature vibrate empathically. While the poet does suffer disharmony, he remains allied to a nature that closely mirrors his sentiments.

Yet, this alliance with nature is not constant, for a large body of poems reveal a decided cleavage between man and nature. In these moments, the disharmony man suffers internally is further exacerbated by his alienation or distance from a harmonious natural realm without. With Browning's «All's right with the world» as epigraph, Florit clearly delineates this gulf in «Para terminar» (DTA, 69). Here, man is portrayed as an intruder or alien whose actions violate the harmonious calm of nature. Yet, man need only heed nature's instructive message and open his mind to her formative influence for all to be well with the world:

No, no, si el mundo está bien hecho.

> *Lo que ocurre es que el hombre es el que es malo*
> *(es un decir), malo por lo que mata y asesina;*
> *porque es un dolor mirarlo como bestia*
> *junto a una flor, un árbol, un arroyo*
> *que quisieran decirle, que le dicen*
> *que tiene que hacer paz, la paz que él quiera*
> *para sí.   Pero el hombre no comprende*
> *y sigue en este juego atroz de matarife . . .*

The repetition of this central thesis at the poem's end (. . . el mundo está bien hecho/ El mal hecho es el hombre, son los hombres . . . que no quieren saber ni ~~comprenderlo . . .~~») works in this poem to widen the chasm between nature and human nature.   This dichotimization is again apparent in «En la ciudad grande» (AP, 309).   Here, the turbulent assertions of human nature can only be steadied and corrected when the mind allows itself to be guided by a *natura naturans,* nature in its active and shaping aspect:

> *. . . Con qué triste ansia*
> *la gente camina*
> *y corre por gusto*
> *de correr, sin mira,*
> *¡un minuto menos*
> *que se viene encima!*
> *Como si después,*
> *al llegar el día,*
> *no nos detuvieran*
> *de pronto la prisa.*
> *Como si al correr*
> *sin el sol por guía,*
> *sin sombra de árboles,*
> *sin aire ni brisa,*
> *no nos envolviéramos*
> *en esta neblina*
> *de vahos oscuros*
> *y caras marchitas . . .*

A symbolic transcription of man's struggle to breach this gulf with nature may be encountered in the final verse of «Cuatro canciones,» #2 (AP, 128): «. . . el hoy con la agonía [man's struggle] de los brazos en el fango [human nature] para buscar esrellas» [numinous nature]. again, in «Canto del mar» (AP, 190), the poet's emotions, calmed and composed by the sea's soft influences in stanza four, are unleashed again in stanza five when he removes himself from her shores: «. . . Y fuera de este límite de horizonte redondo,/ lo demás, lo que duele en mitad de las noches,/ lo que clava sus uñas en la noche del alma. . . .» Else-where, the union with a numinous nature, while possible for others, remains unattainable for the poet caught in the grip of nature as flux. This harmonious but mindless fusion of the «other» with nature is begrudgingly admired in «Nocturno I» (AP, 110) and again in «La nieve» (AP, 135).

. . . Y tú tienes el corazón hecho de risas y de fuego
sin más inquietud que esa de despertar al alba
cuando aún está la noche prendida entre los árboles del río.

Se admirará la luz al ver tus ojos deslumbrados;
se admirarán los cielos al ver cómo respondes al color de
una nube . . . («Nocturno I»)

Tú la verás, blanca y brillante.
La tocarás, fría y suave.
Y estará junto a ti sin angustiarte.

La tendrás en la mano, bajo el pie,
frente a los ojos asombrados.
Te dolerá en la piel.   Te hará reír de gozo.

La arrojarás al aire fino del invierno.
Será un tropel de mariposas blancas
después en el recuerdo.

Pero no la tendrás eternamente
como yo, blanca y fría,
bajo el cielo feliz de los veranos. («La nieve»)

In «Para después» (DTA, 45) as in «La nieve,» nature's indifference to the poet's mortality is again felt when the parenthetical allusion to a serene nature stands in jarring contrast to the reality of his death: «. . . un día, allá en el tiempo/ --había sol, el aire estaba quieto--/ se dispuso a morir. . . .» The brevity of human life is compared to the permanence of nature in «De la luz» (AP, 78) studied earlier. Here, light acts as a synecdoque for the eternal verity of nature which contrasts with man's reality as a vanishing trifle. Because man differs from nature essentially, he differs existentially. In «Elegía en primavera» (DTA, 49), the notion of cyclic recurrence in nature is attached to the image of time's «wheel» with the renascence of spring as its inevitable corollary. Renewal is stressed through skillful use of antithesis («se aleja, vuelve»; «días y noches»; «vuelven y van»; «soles y nieves»; «van, llegan»; «se van y vuelven»), in the repetition of «tiempos y tiempos» and in the adverbial phrase «como siempre.» Only man suffers discontinuity and truncation within a predictable natural sphere:

> . . .La rueda
> del año muerde su cola; cual se aleja, vuelve.
> Aun Dios solo en su reino mira cómo
> días y noches van, tiempos y tiempos
> vuelven y van.   Soles y nieves llegan,
> se van y vuelven como siempre.
> Dios de sus soledades se alimenta.
> Sólo el hombre infeliz se queja y sufre
> por la luz que se marcha, y por la aurora.
> Por saberse sin sol en Primavera.

The poet's rupture with nature is often symptomatic of psychological or spiritual malaise. In the poem «El solitario» (DTA, 41), for example, withdrawing from nature's beneficent influence, he burrows deep into an alienating solitude that seals him off from the external medium through which his mind can be healthily governed: «. . . Habrá tal vez estrellas/ Pero el hombre no quiere ni mirar hacia arriba. . . .» The light that is precious to him in moments of recollection and tranquility becomes, in periods of psychological malaise, an unwelcome intruder: «. . . por el camino caminar sin ver . . . con esta triste claridad . . . me duelen tanto las espinas del alba . . .» (AP, 113).

The anguish that is a part of human nature can act to disconnect the poet from the calming influence of a natural order:

> . . . Miras el libro abierto
> y ni te fijas en la página;
> miras al cielo, por alzar los ojos,
> pero no ves ni la nube que pasa;
> miras la flor: no te enamora;
> miras el árbol: no te espanta;
> oyes el ruiseñor entre la noche
> y no comprendes lo que canta . . . (AP, 252)

As opposed to the qualities of nature suggesting order and security, human nature is symbolically equated with the confusion and conflict of the city in a cluster of poems. When unredeemed and unprotected by nature, human nature reverts to directionless frenzy and anxious seeking:

> . . . Y aquí, con las gentes
> ansiosas, perdidas,
> que pasan y pasan,
> y pasan y giran,
> y pasan y apenas
> se ve la sonrisa . . . (AP, 309)

Even the lights of the city suffer impoverishment and disarray:

> . . . Las luces, en esta
> ciudad sumergida,
> qué pobres se ofrecen,
> qué pálidas brillan.
> Con toda la angustia
> de abajo, de arriba,
> de izquierda y derecha,
> se miran perdidas . . .

The barrenness of the city is counterposed with the purity of nature viewed almost as platonic form:

> . . . Como si las flores
> que del puesto gritan
> por un rayo de aire
> con que se revivan,
> no fuesen más bellas

al aire de arriba,
donde se abren, puras,
su color más viva.

Separated geographically from the fundamental beauty and goodness of nature, the city-poet suffers a psychological malaise. The imagined lament of a ship's figurehead in «El mascarón de proa del museo» (AP, 248), which is cut off from the sea and grounded in a museum, closely parallels the poet's rupture with nature and the consequent devitalization suffered by him in the city. The poet's last stanza is especially effective in revealing man's dependency on nature for life support:

> . . . *Yo que rompí los aires y miré las estrellas,*
> *me deslumbré al relámpago, me mojé con la lluvia,*
> *me sequé con el sol de los veranos*
> *y enrojecí a la aurora del invierno,*
> *que fui libre, Señor, como los pájaros,*
> *yo aquí, en la isla sin el mar, perdido,*
> *roto de ayer, cortado de la proa,*
> *sin espuma y coral, sin gaviotas.*
> *Hundido en la penumbra del museo,*
> *seco.*

Because of a dramatic shift of emphasis that begins in the sixth verse, the stanza may be seen as having two parts of five verses each. The «yo» of the first verse establishes at the outset the link between the figurehead's identity and the natural elements referred to («aire,» «estrellas,» «relámpago,» «lluvia»). The onslaught of verbs («rompí,» «miré,» «deslumbré,» «mojé,» «seguí,» «enrojecí») heightens the sense of a vital interaction with nature once ejoyed. A crescendo is reached in the fifth verse which clearly suggests that such a union with nature was and remains a condition for man's liberation from his own nature («fui libre, Señor, como los pájaros»). The final five verses similarly begin with the subject pronoun, but this time to establish a contrasting and sadder reality. Rupture with nature is accentuated by the thrice repeated negative preposition («sin el mar,» «sin espumas,» «sin gaviotas»). The resulting paralysis and diminishment is conveyed by the five participles used adjectivally to describe the «yo» of verse five («perdido,» «roto,» «cortado,» «hundido,» «seco»). By virtue of the spatial disposition of the final word, «seco,» the poet conveys visually a solitude suffered in debarment from nature.

In «Los poetas solos de Manhattan» (AP, 312) the poet's sensitivity to the dehumanization, the unrelieved ugliness, the violence, debasement, and alienation everywhere about him peaks:

> . . . Aquí todos andamos solos y perdidos,
> todos desconocidos
> entre el ruido
> de trenes subterráneos, y de bombas de incendio,
> y de sirenas de ambulancias
> que tratan de salvar a los suicidas
> que se tiran al río desde un puente,
> o a la calle desde su ventana,
> o que abren las llaves del gas,
> o se toman cien pastillas para dormir
> --porque, como no se han encontrado todavía,
> lo que desean es dormir y olvidarse de todo--,
> olvidarse de que nadie se acuerda de ellos,
> de que están solos, terriblemente solos entre la multitud . . .

The reasons for the poet's disquiet and desolation are patently clear: not only does he stand in isolation from his fellows, but he is closed off from nature:

> . . . Lo que pasa,
> mi muy querido Alcides Iznaga,
> es que aquí no hay vicarias,
> ni Castillo de Jagua,
> ni están conmigo mis poetas
> ni mis palmas («Las palmas, ay . . .»)
> ni las aguas azules de la bahía de Cienfuegos
> ni las de la bahía de La Habana . . .

Account is taken of the inevitable disease that human nature creates for itself when estranged from nature. Always, the accent is on the ugliness, the terrifying solitude of city life:

> Nadie sabe por que.   Nadie lo sabe.

Y yo menos que nadie.
Pero hay un aire triste por el mundo.
¿Será el aliento de los muertos
que sube desde donde la ceniza
quiebra su gris oscuro por la tierra?
¿Será el pecado de los asesinos,
más sucio que ese humo
que se desprende de las chimeneas?
¿O el terror de los hombres solitarios
al caminar de noche por las calles?
¿La mirada que sale sin destino
de amor, sin esperanza
de la otra mirada que la encuentre?
Todo en el aire, todo como revolando
sobre un mundo intranquilo y desvelado.
Porque hay un aire triste por el mundo
que nadie sabe bien qué es, pero que existe
para apagar el fuego de las almas
que quisieran vivir a pesar de la muerte.   (DTA, 59)

In «Escuchando la sinfonía pastoral» (DTA, 65), which is framed in New York City, the poet journeys mentally and envisions a purer natural realm:

. . . Pero ocurre que pienso
que más allá de estas paredes, de estos cuadros,
hay flores sin macetas, libres
cual las hojas de yerba del poeta.
Que allá, donde hay más aire,
se ve el cielo mejor y más hermoso.
Y hasta pueden contarse las estrellas
sin tener que asomarse a la ventana
y casi adivinarlas
a través de la bruma y las luces de abajo.
Y aquel correr tranquilo de las aguas
que van entre las piedras
puliéndolas, dejándolas brillantes
como joyas primeras, sin pecado . . .

Yet, these imaginings are disrupted by sudden awareness of nature's savage side, symbolized, here, by death by lightning.

Once again, as in his earlier years, Florit shrinks from immersion in an uncontrollable natural realm: Man is cautioned, in his quest for harmony, to discard those parts of nature too unsettling or close: «. . . que, vaya, que está bien/ esto de estar en casa sin el miedo/ a que nos parta un rayo.» The counterposition, in several poems, of inner and outer spaces, reveals that Florit is ever mindful of those compelling forces that beckon from without:

> . . . Voy a asomarme a la ventana,
> porque la tarde me está llamando. . . .
> Voy a decirle que estoy tranquilo
> haciendo versos en mi cuarto . . .(AP, 271)

> . . . Afuera está el dolor,
> el gozo, el beso, el odio
> y la mentira, y el ardor, y el sueño.
> Pero aquí, junto a ti, [the night]
> envolviendo tu sombra desvaída
> no está más que el silencio.
> Un silencio amoroso
> de palabras ya dichas . . . (AP, 213)

Seen through this prism, the external world connotes the uncertainty of the unknown thereby magnifying the poet's uneasiness. The chasm between him and nature is now self-created. He retreats to a protective enclosure of his own design, an imaginary citadel within whose precincts he can take refuge and comfort: «. . . Lo de afuera está allí./ Mas en mi noche/ lo más es lo de dentro . . .» (DTA, 37).

The poems that have been studied here show that, whether the poet views himself as allied to nature or apart, he associates himself with those natural elements that tend to mirror and confirm his own disquiet.

Notes

1. Dámaso Alonso, *Poetas españoles contemporáneos* (Madrid: Gredos, 1958), pp. 190-191.

2. Plato, *Symposium* (New York: The Liberal Arts Press, 1950), p. 33.

3. José Olivio Jiménez, *Cinco poetas del tiempo* (Madrid: Insula, 1964), p. 141.

4. Eugenio Florit, Prologue to «Niño de ayer,» included in *Antología penúltima,* no page specified.

5. Eugenio Florit, from AP, 66, 68, 201.

6. Dámaso Alonso, «Un poeta y un libro,» *Revista de Occidente,* XXIII, núm. 98 (agosto, 1931), p. 245.

7. See María Castellanos Collins' *Tierra, mar y cielo en la poesía de Eugenio Florit* (Miami: Ediciones Universal, Colección Polymita, 1976), published since the completion of this manuscript, for a careful study of nature in Florit's poetry.

CHAPTER IV

THE STRUGGLE FOR SERENITY:ANGLES OF VISION

An Art of Recollection

The rounds of pains, longings, and apprehensions that articulate Eugenio Florit's inner life have been studied in Chapter III of this study. A consideration of the poet's quest for serenity in the present and following sections does not imply either chronology or resolution of struggle, but rather points to alternative ways in which Florit responds to his existential situation. It is our intention to show how the adoption of certain angles of vision allows the poet to engage in a «right» seeing that fosters harmony and control.

In his poetry, Florit weaves a dialectical pattern of withdrawal and return from life's arena thus alternating between an art of forgetting, the sidestep that diverts him from the path of a difficult present, as already seen, and an art of recollection involving the refashioning of the past. Here, like Wordsworth, Florit draws on emotions recollected in tranquility. While the poet's memory bank is selective, tending primarily to store serene and happy moments of the past, all experience--when placed at a distance in time--is subject to idealizing revisions. The poetization of the past and its restorative powers over the present is clearly transmitted via the revivifying images of the poem «Recuerdos» (AP, 291):

> . . . Pero hay horas, así, como esta tarde,
> en que un cielo, un color, unas palomas
> nos llevan a pensar en lo distante;
> en lo que, bajo el sol, nos mantenía. . . .
> Que en el recuerdo vienen luz, perfume,
> y que sentimos algo

como un agua de río que nos llega
y nos inunda el corazón
de sombra grata, de frescura verde; . . .

Nature is evoked and valued insofar as it is yoked to remembrance of a happy past:

. . . Aún el ruido del mar, ya tan lejano,
parece resonar cerca, trayendo
con él lo ya perdido
que recupera su presencia . . . (AP, 352)

In Florit's art of recollection, intense feelings are weakened by the length of their journey to the present. The loss of impact through retrospection is analogized metaphorically to elements of nature in «Estatua II» (AP, 109). With the reference to «cada sol hundido en los arroyos/ de mi recuerdo,» the icy waters of the symbolic «arroyos» of memory act as symbolizandum to the extinguishing of passion represented by the sun. Again, in «Momento IV» (AP, 218), the plastic and thermic changes suffered by the sun's rays when reflected on the surface of the sea are likened to the modifications wrought by memory. Or, in «El eterno» (AP, 354), for the poet in absentia, the «terrible» light of the tropics («Terrible luz . . . medrosa por las noches») is softened through tranquil evocation and, together with the sea, is actualized through memory («recuerdo solo, y más, presencia viva»).

As noted under Eros, the poem «Preludio» (AP, 206) serves as a perfect illustration of the function of memory in the poet's quest for harmony. Here, while feelings of love are neither shunned nor suppressed, they are confronted retrospectively. Visually softened, they become a «gris recuerdo.» The nostalgic, idealizing vision of love which contrasts with the present poses no threat to the poet and results in no loss of personal tranquility:

. . . Y ahora que la tarde
por los caminos de la noche pasa;
ahora que tu voz, mujer de entonces,
en otros cielos su ternura muestra,
en la resaca de los años viene
con dolor tu recuerdo apetecido,
y en este cielo de mis nieblas pone

su horizonte de besos . . .

The reference in «Estatua II» (AP, 109) to «besos apagados en el
recuerdo» confirms the efficacy of temporal distance in reducing
feelings to a manageable scale.   Here, as again in the poem
«Las tardes» (AP, 192), the poet feels free to engage in imaginative revisions of a delightful past: «. . . ¡Y qué suave tu recuerdo/
--'no se sabe si viene o si van'--/ con las palomas y la tarde!»
The role of memory in achieving tranquility, e.g. returning him
to life's arena, yet shielding him from risk or impairment, is clear
to the poet: «. . . Sabes que estás en paz con tus recuerdos . . .»
(DTA, 57).

An equally important function of memory is seemingly that
of retarding flux.   In the poem «Otra canción para leer» (AP, 70),
the acute awareness of life's running down (here, the flower's
perishability) is tempered by recollection which ultimately frees
the poet for reaffirmation.   Again, in «Presencia» (AP, 352), the
past reactualized through memory appears to stay the course of
time:

> *. . . la que una vez fue y se repite*
> *ahora, llena de voz suave*
> *sobre una tierra seca . . ,*
> *y lo lejano, apenas visto*
> *en la nostalgia,*
> *recobra su color, y se define . . .*

This belief acts as the poet's consolation as his trepidation is
transmuted into renewal of hope: «Y ya todo está bien, todo
afirmado/ en la cálida sangre verdadera.»

That even death's sting may be healed by memory is the
hopeful message, as already noted, of «Conversación a mi padre»
(AP, 234).   Here, the «survival»-after-death of·the poet's father is
linked to the constant remembrance of him in life by his survivors.

At the extreme end of the spectrum are those feelings which
are so buried that they cannot be called up at will («. . . Claro que
hay más recuerdos . . . y algunos olvidados/ como se olvidan
luego/ los suspiros que damos,/ las palabras de amor,» AP, 268),
or so weakened by time as to become meaningless («. . . Entre las
páginas del libro/ se quedó el nombre disecado./   Cuando lo
abrí para mirar/ se me cayó entre las manos,» AP, 271).

Memories, of course, are not always beneficent. The poem «Asonante final» (AP, 266) shows how past anxieties stored in hidden corners of the mind, are freed in an oneiric context, to surface and to torment anew. The poet begins by eagerly evoking tranquil moments of the past: «. . . Claro que hay más recuerdos/ y todos recordados;/ casi todos serenos. . . .» Yet, within the same poem the poet freely acknowledges that, on a subconscious level, memories are not always subject to repression or to selective control. Instead, they become the «ratoncitos» of the poet's nocturnal phantasmagory which crowd him and gnaw with teeth that cut and tear at the past:

> Claro que hay más recuerdos . . .
> . . . por las noches van saliendo
> como ratoncitos de todos los rincones del silencio
> y llegan, suben, se alzan y me inundan
> con grises aguas, dientes menuditos
> y pedazos de ayer entre las patas . . .

Yet, though there be some polarization even within memory's precinct, distance from the moment remains an effective if not unassailable bridge to serenity.

Childhood: The Return to Eden

In his art of recollection, the poet is not always content with nostalgic backward glances and often yearns to palpably re-experience chapters of the past most free of the contamination and the stress of adult human life. In a large body of poems, by assuming the angle of vision of childhood, Florit is, in fact, successful in enacting such a psychological return to the spiritual innocence and to the serenity of his early years.

The fourteen poems that comprise the collection «Niño de ayer» (1940) view reality almost entirely through the prism of childhood and they unfold in an Edenic setting bearing implications of innocence, freedom, and spontaneity. The prefatory remarks are articulated by the adult poet: fashioned with the wisdom of hindsight, they trace the finite boundaries of life («soñar» to «morir») and acknowledge death's certain infiltratrion of life's terrain: «Luego la muerte se va entrando, nos va destruyendo, absorbiendo, poseyendo, hasta el beso último.» Yet, within the body of poems per se, through mental elipsis, the poet relives the early dreams of childhood.

The sea of the collection's first poem, «El mar» (149), is viewed by the child at a safe distance («De niño, en la montaña,/ estaba el mar desde lo alto/ azul, manso en sus orilla . . .»), and gives symbolic expression to the nature of Eden; just as it is enclosed by the mountains, its waters tame and clear of impurities, so is the child held safe and protected, in joyous union with a beneficent cosmos. While this notion of containment speaks primarily to psychological attitude and state of mind, it is further strengthened by stylistic and structural controls. Beginnings and endings of poems in this collection, for example, are often symmetrical, thereby expressing within their corpus the parameters of a safe and definable universe. The child's angle of vision, moreover, is sustained and complemented by the simplicity of lexicon and syntax.

References to the mountains and seascape of his childhood are not confined to «Niño de ayer,» but find expression in other poems which, spanning a thirty year period, reveal the vividness with which childhood is etched in his memory: «. . . ay, y quiere volver el pensamiento/ a mirar sus montañas y sus mares . . .» (AP, 291); «[the sea] te vió entrar en sus amor cuando era manso/ encerrado en su cerco de montañas severas . . .» (AP, 354); «. . . Venir pasando desde lejos/ cuando era el mar y la montaña/ y no sentíamos que las tardes/ nos angustiaron . . .» (AP, 355). As suggested by the last excerpt, the child's world is characterized by an absence of anguish and by a sense of oneness with nature. Reality is recorded with freshness of perception and felt with a sense of immediacy. This immediacy signifies experience simply given and simply had before the onset of reflection: life as it is before it doubles back on itself in the mediation of self-consciousness. The first stanza of «El mar» (AP, 149), placed within utopic time, captures the harmonious oneness with a sea that simply *is*. In the second stanza, however, the child's vision is contrasted by the adult's philosophical mind: entry is made into historic time and self-conscious reflection. Cognition and historicity alter the poet's response to the sea:

. . . Ahora ya sé que en las espumas

> *despedazado el mar tenía*
> *voz de Ulises y nácar de su Venus;*
> *ahora lo voy soñando con sus pinos,*
> *con el recuerdo*
> *de haber tenido en brazos las galeras de Roma . . .*

If nature be opposed to the reflexive operation of maturity and freedom, then man's immediacy is what he is «by nature.» The adult poet would like to attain the «minimal» existence level of a passive nature which doesn't cognize its mortality: «Hay que pasar como los días/ como las nubes por el cielo . . .» (AP, 355). By emulating nature man can, perhaps, cancel out existential doubt and anchor himself in the present tense, in the moment.   Yet, the poet is aware that man's dialectic nature destroys the innocence he mourns and finally makes impossible the repetition he yearns for--except in the Eden of childhood: within this haven, existential plenitude and immediacy of response, unimpoverished by contingency, can be experienced.

In the poem « El niño en la montaña» (AP, 156), oneness with nature is enriched by keen sensorial awareness:

> *Cuando el niño subía a la montaña*
> *donde viven la águilas,*
> *se sentaba en la cumbre*
> *y dejaba pasar sobre sus ojos*
> *el algodón aéreo de las nubes.*
> *Con aire sin color se despeinaba*
> *su cabeza; perfume*
> *de romero florido*
> *adornaba su ropa;*
> *se llenaba su oído*
> *de esquilas, y balidos*
> *de ovejas, y ladridas*
> *del perro del pastor . . .*

The child's departure from the mountaintop does not mean withdrawal or separation from nature for he carries the essence of its beauty locked within him:

> *. . . Cuando el niño dejaba la montaña*
> *donde viven las águilas,*

> *toda la primavera de la altura*
> *entrábase con él dentro de casa.*

Uncorrupted by civilization («. . . lejos de la Ciudad,/ cerca del mar azul, en sus montañas,» AP, 158) and safe from pain or stress («. . . Ajeno de temor y de cuidado,» AP, 268), the child of nature draws beauty from the spirit of goodness immanent in the scenery.   The conception of nature, as in the verses of «Asonante final» (AP, 266) is often sentimental, religious, or Arcadian:

> *. . .Qué dulce el resbalar de las estrellas,*
> *de las flores de Dios hacia el poniente*
> *de un cielo de verano*
>
> *en el que desde aquellas*
> *horas de soledad el niño ardiente*
> *las iba desclavando en la mano . . .*

The poem «Astronomía,» again of «Niño de ayer» (AP, 163), suggests the union with the kindly beauty of the cosmos and denotes the natural interplay of the objective and the subjective that is the privilege of childhood.   Here, the «niño feliz» (e.g., untouched by the hurt and sorrow of life) contemplates the «cielo tranquilo de verano»--both objective reality and metaphoric expression of Eden.   The actual and the ideal are fused: the child is in harmony with nature and with his own «nature»--«dueño del cielo de su fantasía.»

The Arcadian garden described in «El jardín» (AP, 152) bears all the distinguishing features of the ideal and idealized realm:

Era entre la montaña y el torrente	(Enclosed yet fertile)
reino del crisantemo y la violeta.	(In full flower)
Pequeñito y alegre,	(Self-contained, without sorrow)
niño jardín al borde del camino . . .	(Outside the orbit of time, hence incorruptible. At the

edge of the path leading man
out of Eden to his fall)

Here nature is reliable and steadfast, thereby affording reassurance: «. . . Siempre nos recibía/ el alma en flor de sus enredaderas. . . .»

Nostalgia of Eden, symbolized by the same garden is again expressed in «El recuerdo II» (AP, 201) written one year later. Zigzagging from the present to the past, as memories become «palpably» real, the poet seizes on nature as a point of departure to to effect an elliptical jump to childhood. The interfusion of past and present is accentuated as the poet moves from antithesis («estos,» «aquellos») to synthesis («tú sol, eres el mismo;/ y tú, cielo azul y alto,/ el mismo»).

> *Tan cerca estás, jardín mío,*
> *que casi te voy tocando*
> *al tocar en estos árboles*
> *mis recuerdos de muchacho.*
> *Estas son las flores; éstas*
> *las hojas de aquellos álamos*
> *y éstas las humildes yerbas*
> *que mis nuevos pies pisaron.*
> *Vuelvo a mirar, como ayer,*
> *aquellos lirios morados*
> *y el aliento se me escapa*
> *como ayer en los vilanos.*
> *Y tú, sol, eres el mismo;*
> *y tú, cielo azul y alto,*
> *el mismo que me miraba*
> *junto a los pinos jugando . . .*

The three dimensions of time appear to surrender to an illusion of an eternal, Edenic present. The final verses of the poem sanctify the sublime, carefree purity of childhood in references closely reminiscent of the earlier garden poem (e.g., «alegre»--«feliz»; «camino de mis sueños de muchacho»; «al borde del camino»):

> *Quiero decirte, jardín,*
> *cómo aún te estoy mirando*
> *alegre, junto el camino*
> *de mis sueños de muchacho,*

> *cuando sobre el corazón,*
> *la mariposa y el nardo,*
> *la luz del cielo era limpia*
> *y los pensamientos, claros.*

Beyond a oneness with nature, the childhood of Eden must be understood primarily as a state of mind. In poems such as «Hijo de trapo,» «La novia,» «El nacimiento,» «El maestro Rosa,» and others of «Niño de ayer,» what the reader carries away is the spiritual virginity, the trusting openness to love, the freshness of perception of the child's mind.

In two of Florit's most brilliant poems, «Tarde presente» and «La niña nueva» (AP, 171, 173), an adult viewpoint is brought to bear on the nostalgic vision of Eden. Perhaps the most moving and eloquent of the two is the key poem «Tarde presente» whose very title discloses that it has been wrought in defiance of the substance of time. Liberated by his own thought processes from an enslavement to contingency and to historic time, the poet imagines a tabula rasa, and experiences a miraculous *redintegratio ad statum pristinum:*

> *. . .Como ascensión de un pensamiento libre*
> *hasta el principio*
> *donde nació la luz y se formaron*
> *entraña de dolor, germen de grito*
> *y lágrima primera bajo el cielo . . .*

Within the sanctuary of Eden that the poet divines, time, death, and sorrow have no entry and life-forces flourish, renewed and pure. To facilitate poetic visualization, time is first made to halt («Como si detenido el tiempo»). Then, the three *ec-stases* of time fuse into an Edenic present where meaning is revealed in plenitude and oneness: «. . . Como si ayer llegara . . . y mañana estuviera ya . . . como si hoy fuera una enorme rosa/ de millones de pétalos unidos/ en una sola esquina del mundo revelado. . . .» Hence, the thousand petals are as one; in the existential immediacy of experience no fragmentation or loss of unity occurs. Historic time is erased and, with it, all sorrow known to man: «. . . Como si Dios en su alto pensamiento/ secara el llanto de sus hijos. . . .» Death is halted and infinite renewal, miraculous continuance are assured:

> . . . y Ella, la sin color, durmiera al borde florecido
> de sus innumerables tumbas . . .
> Como si todo junto de repente
> se pusiera entre el hombre y su destino.
> Como si ante el ocaso rojo abriera
> un girasol sus rayos amarillos.
> Como si aquella mano
> de ayer regara azules lirios
> y fuera el mar bajo la mano
> un palomar de pétalos heridos.
> Y como si los barcos emergieran
> de su muerte de hierros, de su sueño
> de peces, de su olvido,
> para tender sus velas inmortales
> a los vientos y al sol . . .

In this Arcadia, life is kindled anew and embraced with fresh innocence and jubilation:

> . . . Como si fríos
> los huesos de la tierra,
> por fuego inmaterial enrojecidos
> hasta el blanco del alma
> volvieran a pesar, a estremecerse,
> a reír y a llorar en risa y llanto
> de verdad, en latidos
> de pecho verdadero, en ojos limpios,
> en bocas sin pecado, en tibia
> caricia de sus carnes . . .

The association of childhood with lost innocence and with yearned for immediacy is again made clear in the poem «La niña nueva.» Here, the angle of vision, however, is that of the adult poet who in a poetic dialogue which is, in fact, an interior monologue, expresses painful awareness of the existential gulf that separates him from the newborn child he beholds. Here Florit appears to draw heavily on the Platonic myth of the child's pre-existence in a Heaven where eternity, permanence, and essential truths abide. The heavenly atmosphere from whence the child comes, however, cannot be maintained on earth and thus the child becomes an exile or alien, losing the joyful sense of reconciliation with nature. Innocence is replaced by a reflexive complexity that calls into question the meaning and purpose of existence («viene tu pregunta, hecha ya tú»). Man's ontological questions are slated to remain unanswered:

> Ya entre nosotros, forma verdadera,
> pequeña realidad de sangre viva,
> aún con el asombro,
> con la inquietud aún
> de no saber por qué llegaste.
> Y no habrás de saberlo ya jamás
> aunque desplieguen a tu vista
> sus vuelos serafines
> y Dios se te revele en una rosa,
> y en una tarde el mundo se te entregue.
> No la sabrás. Y llorarás de pena,
> y reirás, y tendrás el alma a flor de piel,
> y amarás unos ojos,
> y besarás labios de vida y muerte.
> Pero no lo sabrás.
>
> Tu viaje aquí,
> va dentro del misterio de las músicas
> que vuelan de astro en astro,
> de cielo en cielo,
> de corazon en corazón.
> Y viene tu pregunta
> hecha ya tú . . .

Basking in the aura of innocence and harmony the newborn child carries from a heavenly life at which he can only guess («. . . La nube en que dormiste,/ tu sueño de molécula de luz . . .»), the poet feels more keenly the ravages of his soul, his «sorge» or anxious dread:

> . . .Porque te miro y me da miedo
> que me mires el alma empedernida,
> tú que la tienes frágil, pura, aérea
> --una llamita que sostiene apenas
> el ansia de más viva llamarada . . .

Unlike the poet's ontological solitude and alienation («que vivo/ este sueño de ausencia atormentada»), the child is at one with herself («el pensamiento que eras en tu sueño»). The poet expresses a final longing to be reintegrated and at one with that former state of harmonious pre-existence:

> *. . . Y cuando sepas que te vi durmiendo,*
> *y, despierta, te quise preguntar*
> *el color de tu nube,*
> *la luz en que soñabas,*
> *el pensamiento que eras en tu sueño,*
> *me llorarás a mí, que vivo*
> *este sueño de ausencia atormentada*
> *por volver a mi nube,*
> *a mi átomo de tierra:*
> *a mi definitiva presencia entre la nada.*

Yet, as with the child's birth into the precariousness of earthly life in «La niña nueva,» the sojourn in Eden is short-lived and man's exit is clearly prescribed. Therefore, as the poem «El jardín» reminds us at its close, the poet cannot make his way back permanently to the cherished garden of his memory. Such a possibility is foreclosed, by implication: «Si hoy, como aquella vez, pudiera, iría.» As in the poem, the «storm» of time lays permanent waste to the garden. Similarly, the azure clarity of the metaphoric «sea» of childhood («El mar,» AP, 149) gives way to the protean, multi-colored waters that capture the permutations and uncertainty of lived experience.

Perhaps it is the final poem of the collection of *Niño de ayer* that most graphically and poignantly traces rupture and exile from Eden. Unlike the introductory poem, «El mar» where the sea is viewed from afar, this poem is significantly entitled «Un barco sobre el mar (AP, 167). Here, the child boards the metaphoric bark of life and hazards, at last, those turbulent waters which carry him on fluid and irresistible pathways to the center of himself. The exit from the sanctuary of childhood (described in the first stanza) is accompanied by the first barbs of sorrow («y unas lágrimas tristes le rodaron»). In the final stanza the child is «born» to earthly life and, alone, confronts the contingent path of freedom:

Un día de verano
el niño aquel se despidió sin lágrimas
del pueblo que fue suyo
durante nueve años.
Allí quedaba toda
su vida pequeñita:
el balompié, la bicicleta,
los patines y el aro;
se quedaba el jardín
con sus violetas y sus crisantemos;
el maestro y la novia; los amigos
quedaban en su puesto.
Pero el niño, aquel día de verano
se despidió sin lágrimas,
con la ilusión puesta en el barco
que iba a llevarlo lejos . . .

Sólo cuando el vapor
comenzó a despegarse de su muelle
y la Ciudad se iba quedando
mientras él se marchaba,
los ojos de aquel niño
brillaron más que nunca
y unas lágrimas tristes le rodaron
y cayeron al mar . . .

Durante muchos días
llenos de cielo y agua
fue el niño aquel naciendo en su viaje,
y aprendió a estar de noche.
solo frente a la luna,
viendo cómo la proa de su barco
le marcaba un camino hacia poniente...

Disquiet Quelled Through Art

We are concerned, here, with identifying the ways in which Florit's craft enables him to exorcize his demons and realize a measure of harmony. In pursuing this question, we find that the early articles «Una hora conmigo» and «Regreso a la serenidad» still serve as convenient guideposts and represent entrenched if opposing views regarding the nature of art.

In the first, «Una hora conmigo,» dark and uncontrolled impulses are openly acknowledged and clarified through art which therefore serves an importance therapeutic function. This belief is ratified by Florit in a number of subsequent writings. In «El poema» (AP, 252), the epigraph taken from Robert Frost, «A poem begins with a lump in the throat,» indicates straightaway that, here, it is emotion that activates poetic process. Desirous of pinpointing and defining diffuse feelings, the poet has recourse to a series of comparisons which act as objective correlatives of emotion:

> ... No se te calma el nudo ni la angustia,
> que es como si todo un cielo se te hundiera,
> o como si nadando por el agua
> con las flores del agua te enredaras.
> Como soñar que vas cayendo,
> yendo cayendo que caerás sin prisa
> y que nadie te espera al fin de la caída ...

The difficulties of externalizing feelings are cognized: «. . . Es como que te ahoga un pensamiento/ que quiere hablar, salir, saltar, volar,/ y cada vez da con la jaula . . .»), yet, the very act of setting them to paper serves to free the poet of them. Through the introspection required of all creation, the sequence emotion-thought-poem can be enacted:

> ... Has de volver a ti las soledades
> con que vas habitando tus moradas,
> y pensar poco a poco el pensamiento,
> y decir poco a poco las palabras,
> y formar el poema con la angustia
> que te mordía la garganta.

We are again alerted to this truth in the verses of «Pude escribir» (AP, 346) where desires are subdued through poetry: «Pude escribir mi espera en la esperanza/ que una vez se me puso enfrente/ para aquietarme un poco los anhelos. . . .»

The poems «Asonante final» (AP, 266) and «Lo otro» (DTA,

27) again make candid a poetic credo which appears to stress the passionate, uncontrolled side of inspiration which is in need of an ordering context. Yet, before feelings can materialize as verse, there is a whole state that is prior and which borrows closely from a vocabulary of gestation. In the process of creation, seeds of possibility take on life and shape:

> . . . *porque a veces es la palabra como un*
>   *aliento sobrehumano*
> *que nos sube a la garganta --¿de dónde Señor?--*
>   *y si no hablamos*
> *nos quedaríamos ahogados.*
> *¿De dónde, Señor?   ¿De qué rincón de la sangre,*
>   *de qué pliegue del alma . . .*
>
> *que no quiere llegar pero está dentro.*
> *¿Se sabrá alguna vez cómo, cuándo comienza a arder?*
> *¿Sabremos en qué oscuro rincón se combinan las letras*
> *para luego salir hechas palabras? . . .* («*Lo otro*»)

The unexpressed word is like the unborn child that lies passively *in utero*. It must be energized, set free, for life is tied to the word: «. . . Palabra enmusgada, quieta, dormida, muerta./ No. Tiene que salir, rodar, rodar, hablar, hablar, hablar./ Al principio fue el verbo . . .» (AP, 272). Once fully formed, feelings are expelled and born as poems:

> . . . *porque me está quemando*
> *dentro de mí la sangre de su alma;*
> *la carne de su idea*
> *nada bajo un montón de pensamientos,*
> *quiere salir al sol, alza los brazos*
> *y muestra en los cabellos como estrellas*
> *gotas de agua fulgurando . . .* (AP, 266)

Again, in «Asonante final» and in «A la poesía» (AP, 321) feelings are regulated by the intellect. In the first of these poems, the diffuse emotion at the poem's start is ultimately focused and directed to a search for «el pensamiento» at the poem's end:

«. . . digo que busco, que te busco a tí, mi pensamiento. . . .»

A similar sequence is suggested in «A la poesía»:   «. . . Mira que estoy a recibirte/ con el ardor del que te sueña;/ que pienso y pienso, por si pensando/ pudiera alguna vez, pudiera. . . .» Art, then, serving as a cathartic agent can quell disquiet in a collaborative engagement of reason and emotion. It is the cognition of this interaction that lends special interest, first to the article «Una hora conmigo» and then to those poems that illustrate it.

«Regreso a la serenidad,» instead, shows that serenity may also be secured by curtailment of such interaction or even by denial of emotion.   As noted earlier in this study, the article equates the return to serenity with the «rediscovery» of classic norms stressing reason, intelligence, and purity of form.   Feelings, consequently, are chastened, channeled, or suppressed. As demonstrated in Chapter II («A poetry of Outwardness»), the poet marshals the resources of the spirit and actively constructs his own images of serenity in a «pure» poetry characterized by artistic measure and restraint.   The essence of this poetry, redefined by Florit in 1944 in «La poesía (AP, 357), is found to rest with the interface of reason and harmony: «Una rama del aire que se mece/ a la pausa del viento verdadero,/ hecha de dulce resonar/ y de armonioso pensamiento. . . .»   Similarly, the tribute paid to Platonic thought and to the view of art as imitation of nature in «Regreso a la serenidad» is ratified subsequently in the poem «Lo otro» (DTA, 27).   Written forty years later, it bespeaks continued if not unswerving commitment to classic precepts: «. . . ¿Es posible empezar algo nuevo?/ La rosa fue creada aun antes que el poema/ Y nadie, nunca, nunca/ escribirá un poema mejor. . . .»

In his pursuit of a harmony modeled on classic beauty, Florit is not reliant on internal inspiration alone for, within other modalities of art, he also finds reliable images of transcendent serenity.   Indeed, Florit frequently turns to sculpture and painting, drawn to them for the sense of permanence they convey. The beautifully chiseled verses of «Estrofas a una estatua» (AP, 107) describe a statue which epitomizes, quintessentially, the impermeable serenity, the unflawed perfection of art.   Placed within art's eternal sphere, the statue stands outside the orbits of time, pain, or reverie («inmóvil,» «la pupila ciega,» «No has de sentir cómo la luz se muere,» «desnuda de memorias y de lágrimas,» «donde ya no se sueña»). The poet admires her purity and form («naciste para estar pura,» «tu perfecta geometría») and is uplifted and steadied («Qué serena ilusión tienes, estatua/ de eternidad bajo la clara noche»).

Monumento ceñido
de un tiempo tan lejano de tu muerte.
Así te estás inmóvil a la orilla
de este sol que se fuga en mariposas.

Tú, estatua blanca, rosa de alabastro,
naciste para estar pura en la tierra
con un dosel de ramas olorosas
y la pupila ciega bajo el cielo.

No has de sentir cómo la luz se muere
sino por el color que en ti resbala
y el frío que se prende a tus rodillas
húmedas del silencio de la tarde.

Cuando en piedra moría la sonrisa
quebró sus alas la dorada abeja
y en el espacio eterno lleva el alma
con recuerdo de mieles y de bocas.

Ya tu perfecta geometría sabe
que es vano el aire y tímido el rocío;
y cómo viene el mar sobre esa arena
con el eco de tantos caracoles.

Beso de estrella, luz para tu frente
desnuda de memorias y de lágrimas;
qué firme superficie de alabastro
donde ya no se sueña.

Por la rama caída hasta tus hombros
bajó el canto de un pájaro a besarte.
Qué serena ilusión, tienes, estatua,
de eternidad bajo la clara noche.

In «Retrato» (AP, 132) Florit is again inspired by a model of classic grace. The uncompromised perfection of the portrait bespeaks, as phrased by Shelley, a form «more real than living man.» The adjectives «perfecto,» «bello,» appearing sequentially three times (once in transposition) are the attributes most admired and most emphasized by the poet. Other descriptive details of the portrait («. . . sin sombra en las pupilas verdes»; «. . . el transparente nácar de la túnica . . .») also promote the illusion of harmonious clarity symbolizing a transcendent serenity:

> Estaba allí, perfecta, bella,
> sin sombra en las pupilas verdes.
> El oro, de corona; el transparente nácar,
> de túnica; la sonrisa, de aureola.
> Bella, perfecta, en pura geometría
> de mármol y caricia de sol último.
> ¿Qué pensamiento, bajo la amplia frente?
> ¿Qué beso, al borde de los labios?
> ¿Qué imagen, tras los ojos detenidos
> en una mariposa del espacio?
> Allí, perfecta, bella.   Entre los dedos
> un alma de paloma muerta
> luchaba por entrarse hasta su sangre
> y anidar otra vez bajo su seno.

> En torno el ángel de la música
> se iba en ocaso, al mar, desvaneciendo.

While the poem «Estatua II» (AP, 109) provokes a return to a more impassioned realm, the imagery of the last stanza suggests that feelings called forth in contemplation of the statue are subdued contemporaneously by association with the perfection and control of its sculptural form: «Tenías el ardor de las palomas/ de mármol, en las fuentes del otoño./   clara estatua de besos apagados/ en el recuerdo. . . .»

As a writer actively exercising his craft, Florit frequently succeeds in reversing the foreboding and disquiet caused by awareness of flux and finitude.   In part, it is this very awareness that impels him to record the poetic message straightaway: «. . . hay que decirlo ahora,/ hay que cantar cuando aún hay canto/

y decírnoslo mientras que podemos . . .» (AP, 266).   However, through his art, and the permanence it insures, Florit succeeds in freeing himself, in part, from his bondage to time.   That time is, in fact, imprisoned by the written word is intimated abstractly in «Tarde presente» (AP, 271):   «. . . Como si ayer llegara con su recuerdo escrito/ y mañana estuviera ya en su cárcel de letras. . . .»

Central to the arrival at serenity through art is the belief held by Florit that his essential being is caught and held in his work.   In «Una hora conmigo» he rejects the dichotimization of «poetizar-ser» for, in his view, they are one and the same: «. . . Pero es que el poeta mientras poetiza ¿no está siendo?   ¿Es que para ser es preciso no poetizar?   El hombre en trance de poesía vive un mundo suyo . . . en él, es como su verdad le obliga a ser. . . .»

The poetic object, with the preternatural vivacity that is induced by art, testifies to his existence.   In the *Deo gratia* of «Asonante final,» the poet yokes the gift of poetry with that of being:

> . . . *Revelación que Dios nos hace en un momento*
> *cuando a las cinco de la tarde*
> *todo mi mundo está en silencio*
> *para que pueda resonar más en lo hondo*
> *el sonido de la máquina de escribir*
> *que está escribiendo esta palabra*
> *que ahora en este minuto estoy creando.*
> *Ella está, y yo estoy.   Escribiendo, creando.*
> *Dios mío, gracias por haberme dado*
> *la máquina y los dedos,*
> *y la hoja de papel,*
> *y la palabra en que se abre el pensamiento.*
> *Gracias por dejarme estar, dejarme ser . . .*

The writer's evolving perception of reality is translated into a poetic language which expresses the essential unicity of his being:

> . . . *No es igual la palabra aunque sea la misma*
> *Como no soy igual a ayer, como no lo es mi sangre*
> *aunque sean iguales las palabras.*

> *No es lo mismo esto que escribo ahora*
> *que lo que otros escribieron antes.   Aunque sea lo mismo*
> *No lo es.   Porque es otra la sangre.*
> *Y otro el misterio en cada uno.   Como es otra*
>   *la muerte.* (DTA, 27-28)

> *. . .Pero hay que decirlo ahora . . . .*
> *Como ya se lo han dicho tantos,*
> *aunque de otra manera, de la mía,*
> *que es como yo quiero declararlo . . .* (AP, 266)

That poetry testifies to the poet's existence as well as to his uniqueness is evident in such poems as «A mi mano» (AP, 244), «Ansia de Dioses» (AP, 332), «Lo que queda» (DTA, 53), «El hombre solo» (AP, 342), and «Asonante Final» (AP, 266).   In the first of these, «A mi mano,» the poet anticipates that his work will serve as a bridge to eternity, and resolves to express himself sincerely:

> *. . .Pinta las buenas, las elocuentes;*
> *di las palabras como las sientes;*
> *clava las letras según las viste,*

> *para que al menos cuando te mueras*
> *dejes al mundo, de lo que eras,*
> *las formas fijas de lo que fuiste.*

The remaining poems view art through the prism of death. Through his poetry, Florit assays a mediation between eternal and mortal poles of orientation.   In «Para empezar» (DTA, 23), for example, his words attest to his actuality and stand as proof that he is: «Para empezar tan sólo.   Para decir que aún estoy vivo/ en esta noche solo. . . .»   Existence is played off against essence in a citational, antiphonal process.   The poet affirms his essential being through his verses even as existence ceases.   In «Ansia de Dioses,» he is the «pobre dios mortal» who makes an impassioned plea that his verses not be forgotten.   Borrowing from the tenets of idealist philosophy, the poet implies that his verses will cease to exist (and with them his being) if they are not read.   The revivification of the poems and the poet are clearly correlated:

«. . . ¿Qué el otro pobre dios mortal/ necesita por aire, de alimento,/ sino saber que alguien detiene/ la mirada en sus versos. . . .» By virtue of his art, the poet can pass from death («su destierro») through the gateway of immortality («seguirse siendo»):

> Ansia de dioses es el homenaje
> para vivir su eternidad contentos.
> Sube el amor, que los ampara,
> como sube el incienso.
>
> ¿Qué el otro pobre dios mortal
> necesita por aire, de alimento,
> sino saber que alguien detiene
> la mirada en sus versos,
> y por amor, con el amor
> va buscándolos dentro,
> para encontrar la luz que tengan,
> y la poca memoria de su cielo
> --del que perdió una vez-- y cada día
> el pobre dios está perdiendo?
>
> ¿Qué otra cosa que ese amor
> necesita el poeta en su destierro?
> ¿Y qué poco --qué mucho-- ¡cuánto mucho!
> para poder seguirse siendo?

In «Asonante final,» «El hombre solo,» and «Lo que queda,» Florit again imagines the eternalization of his essential being through his art. In the first of these, woven from the three strands of time, the poet is in search of «the poem» from the Edenic beginnings, the «versos indecibles» of «Niño de ayer» to the final moment of death when those who mourn him set out to find him in his work, «sobre todas las páginas de mis libros.»

The poet again reflects on his life and his work in the final taking of account of «El hombre solo»: «. . . Cuando me vaya ¿qué? Los pocos versos/ que fui escribiendo al paso de la vida. . . .» The poem «Lo que queda» gives definitive expression to the hope of immortality that sustains him. His disquiet quelled, death's pain can be borne: «. . . Eso no importa./ No importa, porque quedan nuestros versos. . . .»

Art, then, has a central function in Florit's quest, alternately offering him models of classic restraint, channels of self-expression, analogues of transcendent serenity, or lifelines to eternity. With awareness and gratitude, Florit avails himself of its guideposts in charting his difficult course.

Nature as Permanence: The Poet in Harmony

Because Florit expresses himself largely through imagery and symbols drawn from nature, differences in perception and delineation of nature are keystones of the poet's inner life and attest to the continued struggle for accommodation and resolution of dialectical tension.

While Florit's engagement with nature, as noted, is constant, his relationship is variable and may be active or passive, alien or friendly. In nature, Florit alternately encounter a corroboration of his darkest fears and a confirmation of his keenest desires.

Only the controlled universe of *Trópico* is largely untouched by the poet's personal drama. Yet, even the nature of *Trópico* exemplifies a selective viewing of reality which is made to conform to inner need. The reduced parameters and foci of Florit's tropics suggest a correlation between spatial and emotive control which later works bear out.(1)

In Florit's subsequent collections, and contingent on his frame of mind, identical natural forms may suggest opposite things, now depicting flux and disquiet, now permanence and harmony. It is to the latter two images that we now turn our attention.

Florit formulates the desire to engage in «right» seeing in a Wordsworthian sense: «. . . Ay, quién mirara el agua/ por ella misma,/ para estarla mirando/ quieto, sin prisa . . .» (AP, 243). If the psychological basis of this yearning is the desire to perceive the infinite within the finite, it is to nature in its most ennobling and enduring form that Florit turns to fullfill it.

The mind now acts as a filter giving entry only to images of continuity and order. Water which elsewhere stands as a paradigm of flux, bespeaks serenity, renewal, or both:

Constancia: la del río que pasa . . . (AP, 225)

... Aquí están tus colores,, tu sereno misterio;
aquí tu voz antigua presa en las caracolas;
aquí la risa eterna del claro pensamiento ... (AP, 190)

... ¡Cómo ha de estar viva
de plata, serena
y henchida
de luz alta, celeste ... (AP, 242)

... Vienen las olas
rizando su copete, deslizándolo
en giros desiguales, y seguras
de su destino de acabar, volviendo
a su eterno moverse, en la serena
ordenación del mar que nunca cesa ... (DTA, 35)

Nature repeatedly exemplifies stability and eternal recurrence.
In its obliviousness to time and its surety of renewal it embodies
in «Seguro pensamiento» (AP, 216) an existential ideal from which
the poet draws strength:

Estas noches así basta la luna
que redonda en su luz sube a los altos cielos
sin prisa, tan segura
de brillar y morir, para mañana
volver sobre este cielo en que la vemos.

Nos basta, a veces, con mirar un árbol
estas noches así, trémulo y solo,
tan seguro de hojas y de pájaros
y de un beso del sol a la mañana;
de renacer a cada primavera.

A veces basta la hojita de yerba
--la humilde-- en el camino
por donde ni nos vamos ni volvemos.
y que está allí, segura
de su destino.

Estas noches así basta el silencio
sobre la tierra sorda;

basta, para pensar que estamos vivos,
mirar al cielo
y recordar palabras olvidadas:
misterio, astros, universo, alma.

Estas noches así, después del viaje
de las sombras en lo ancho de la tierra,
qué inútiles parecen
y qué perdidas las demás palabras.

When the concept of cyclic recurrence, reminiscent of Heraclitean laws of exchange, is brought to bear on the reality of death, faith is placed in renascence which triumphs over finality and dispair:(2)

. . . Y la muerte que huele a primavera . . . (AP, 219)

. . . Aquí, el ayer con su vendimia de muertes florecidas
y el mañana con su promesa de raíces . . . (AP, 128)

. . . Bajo la frente blanca de la tierra,
¡qué verdes pensamientos para la primavera!. . . (AP, 287)

. . . el aire está lleno de un oro plácido
en el bullir de nueva primavera . . . (AP, 315)

In a line with Orphic doctrine, the poet stresses death as a «rebirth,» a reintegration into the cosmos. This is clearly seen in «Para tu ausencia» (AP, 98), dedicated to the poet's father and which takes as its epigraph Shelley's verses; «Peace, peace, he is not dead, he doth not sleep. He hath awakened from the dream of life.»

Te fuiste aquel minuto para toda la muerte
a navegar en hondos oceanos de silencio
con un largo camino de pupilas dormidas
y un banco de palomas prendido a tus ensueños.

Ya estarás por ausentes claridades de luna,
más tuyo que en las flechas de tu reloj de oro
donde contabas tanto minuto sin orillas

para la sed de alas que quemaba tus hombros.

Y habrás saltado mares que la inquietud miraba,
abismos en la tímida soledad de tu ausencia;
y en la noche habrás sido tenue brisa caliente
junto a aquel pedacito de tu amorosa tierra.

Largo abrazo de alientos sobre las amapolas,
y una risa, y un canto sin palabras ni música;
y un aquí estoy, gozoso de pasados insomnios,
y un para siempre, cálido en la fría llanura.

Como partiste en brazos del silencio apretado
resonará más viva la luz de tus palabras;
y en cada estrofa de aire se enredará un acento,
y en cada mariposa te nacerán más alas.

Gozo de estar yo vivo para el eterno día;
de saberte en el agua, y en el sol, y en la yerba.
Harás entre las nubes Nacimientos de plata
y encontrarás tu nido en un árbol de estrellas.

The poet himself formulates the desire to be reabsorbed into eternal matter in «La niña nueva» (AP, 174):

. . . me llorarás a mí, que vivo
este sueño de ausencia atormentada
por volver a mi nube,
a mi átomo de tierra:
a mi definitiva presencia entre la nada . . .

Again, in «Cuatro canciones,» #4 (AP, 129), in death the poet imagines himself as a part of the eternal interchange of the constituent elements of the cosmos:

Cuando sea la tierra mi pan y mi vino
habré encontrado el sueño para siempre.
Todo un sueño de siglos, de primaveras y de inviernos
que pasarán sobre mis huesos fríos.

Y así estará mi jugo de poeta

> *vertiéndose en regatos interiores*
> *para salir al sol en aguas cristalinas.*

When viewed through this prism, death seems natural and painless: «. . . Todo tendrá la historia/ de un crepúsculo suave de montaña,/ y en el adiós eterno, los adioses/ se dormirán en tumbas de distancia . . .» (AP, 77). Within the calming precinct of nature, the cutting edge of anxiety is effectively blunted and even the much feared water-union of death is portrayed as a desideratum:

> *. . . Qué esperanza de verse azul al doblar la mañana*
> *y navegar sobre las horas infinitas*
> *cuando esté la mano de Dios llamando a su criatura*
> *descelada . . .* (AP, 190)

(Referring to the sea)

> *. . .Desmarado, tenías que volverte hacia él;*
> *ausente, regresar en recuerdo;*
> *muerto, cuando lo estés, en viaje eterno,*
> *ser, sí, ser sobre todo como la luz que se desliza*
> *y en ondas de color prende su beso . . .* (AP, 354)

> *Por sus cruces de hierro ya la sal está blanca.*
> *Así tiende el recuerdo las manos en el cielo*
> *hacia una esquina clara del mar Mediterráneo*
> *con mármoles y yerbas altas para la brisa.*

> *Dulce soñar de huesos húmedos de rocío,*
> *si los ojos aún pueden mirar las velas tensas*
> *cerca del punto suave con cántico de espumas*
> *y el bajo vuelo y el chillar de gaviotas . . .*

> *Mar de siempre, de todos; tan niño, luminoso*
> *por la espuma de una fragante voz eterna,*
> *viene tan cerca y tan amigo de sus muertos*
> *para llorar al sol peces rojos y azules . . .* (AP, 93)

> *Tú no tienes por qué llorar,*
> *ni morir de melancolía.*

> *Sólo tienes que ver pasar*
> *el agua abajo, de río a ría,*
>
> *y esperar a llegar al mar . . .*
> *Que ya entrarás en la mar un día.* (AP, 331)

In a similar sense, the earth is portrayed both as matrix and final shelter:

> *Y si desnudos nos parió ¿qué mucho*
> *que así desnudos nos reciba?*
> *A esta madre no le dolemos,*
> *ni ella nos duele a nosotros, viva.* (AP, 204)
>
> *¡Y qué bien estarías*
> *tú, corazón, dándote todo*
> *en esta tierra firme y plácida!*
>
> *¡Y qué hermosas,*
> *como esta tarde clara,*
> *las hortensias cayendo*
> *hasta besarte el alma!* (AP, 198)

When seen through the angle of vision of permanence and cyclic recurrence, nature bespeaks serenity and calm and its formative influence on the poet is direct, now guiding and soothing, now lifting and inspiring.

When through the interfusion of the real and the ideal the poet's union with nature is effected, he is at last able to experience harmony and to feel himself embraced and cherished by the cosmos. Florit articulates the importance of this harmonious union with nature in a variety of poems which range from the early affirmations of «Nocturno I» of *Doble Acento* to the mature self-assessment of «Biografía» (*Antología penúltima*), and «El amante» (*De tiempo y agonía*). Almost always, in the poet's view, it is the love of nature that most closely defines him:

> *. . .Déjame.   Porque no tengo más amor dentro del pecho*
> *endurecido*
> *que este amor a la tierra, o al mar, o a los vientos, o a las*
> *estrellas apagadas . . .* (AP, 111)

. . .*Aún ama mucho.   El sol, los árboles,*
las primaveras, los inviernos . . . (AP, 353)

. . . El amor a la luz, como el amor hasta a la sombra
A lo que iba: el amor a lo creado, por pequeño que
*   sea . . .* (DTA, 43)

Love implies wonder and praise for all external life. Beyond
these general assertions, discrete aspects of nature (the sea, the
earth, clouds, twilight) to which the poet feels harmoniously
linked, are singled out for special attention. The sea of «El
eterno» (AP, 354), for example, is a living force to which he is
conjoined in life and in death:

No sabías que el mar con sus colores
--verde, amarillo, azul, gris, negro, de la luna--
iba a llegar a poseerte para siempre.
Su orilla pedregosa
tan de ayer y tan lejos,
te vió entrar en su amor cuando era manso
encerrado en su cerco de montañas severas,
y te vió sobre él hacia Occidente.
Iba contigo como sangre.   Voces íntimas
de caracolas te sonaban
en los oídos que luego iban a enmudecerse.
Fue llegando después el mar de las arenas
bajo la luz terrible del Trópico.   Terrible
luz, y tan suave por las tardes.   Medrosa por las noches
cuando a lo negro se lo mira fantasmal.
Para siempre.   Hasta ahora que en su ausencia
es un recuerdo al que una vez se llega
de paso, albatros volandero
de viene y va por aires y distancias.
Recuerdo solo y más, presencia exacta
de su estar, ser, vivir, latir en donde siempre.
Desmarado, tenías que volverte hacia él;
ausente, regresar en recuerdo;
muerto, cuando lo estés, en viaje eterno,
ser, sí, ser sobre todo como la luz que se desliza
y en ondas de color prende su beso.

Absence from the sea represents a loss of plenitude and in 1930 («Mar,» #7) as in 1969, in the just cited poem «El eterno,» Florit feels the need to evoke and actualize it through remembrance:

> Hoy en voces de ausencia
> lejos de ti, por mirarte
> cerca llega de tu parte
> milagro fiel de tu esencia . . .(AP, 53)

The trenchant longing for some linkage to the sea is phrased simply and stirringly in «El deseo» (AP, 261) with the poet's voice, innocent and undemanding, that of the son's to God, the father:

> El mar esta mañana
> me alegra con su sal.
>
> Permite, Señor.   Nada.
> Lo que quieras será.
>
> Pero si acaso, acaso
> me quieres escuchar,
>
> Señor, de vez en cuando
> déjame ver el mar.

In moments of reconciliation with nature, the earth receives special treatment as well. It responds as passionate lover bringing seed to full flower or it is the earth-mother, cherishing and comforting the poet-child in a maternal embrace. By virtue of the mother-child symbolism, the numinous force of nature is made more benevolent:

> Cuando se la quiere da
> todo su amor apasionado
> y pone el alma con su flor
> en la caricia que le damos. (AP, 204, #9)
>
> En la perfecta soledad
> qué caricias nos da la tierra
> cuando la vamos a sembrar. (AP, 204, #7)

Hijo, ya ves cómo la tierra
cada llanto que recibe
la devuelve en la flor nueva. (AP, 205, #10)

. . . A esta madre no le dolemos,
ni ella nos duele a nosotros, viva. (AP, 204, #5)

When the human soul is in harmony with a numinous nature,
it also touches and rests in its spiritual home. In «Canciones
para la soledad,» #4 (AP, 181) love of nature, felt in the peaceful
solitude of dusk, is transmuted into religious emotion: «¡Qué
dulce ya con ella/ mientras la tarde baja/ y se van encendiendo/
las estrellas del alma!»

External nature contributes to the poet's sense of the unity
of all things. The fusion of horizons of sea, land, and sky reflect
Florit's intuition of an organically interconnected universe:

. . . Cerca es el ondular, y más allá, la calma.
Por fin el horizonte estático
unido al cielo fijo, gris, que apenas dibuja
su línea . . . (DTA, 35)

. . .Agua de cielo se reduce
en agua mar y agua laguna . . . (AP, 327)

. . . en esa línea donde están los besos
de las aguas del cielo con las nubes del mar . . . (AP, 175)

. . . Porque el destino tuyo, mar, de muerte y de vida . . .
hay que aprenderlo aquí, frente al ocaso,
cerca de aquella nube que se baña los pies
en el término ansiado de tu rojo horizonte . . . (AP, 190)

Realidad de fuego en frío,
quiébrase el son en cristales
al caer en desiguales
luces sobre el claro río. . . (AP, 47)

[El mar] . . . Encendido
más por el cielo caído
en regular geometría . . . (AP, 51)

> . . . ¡Cómo ha de estar viva
> de plata, serena
> y henchida
> de luz alta, celeste . . . (AP, 242)

> . . .Un cielo limpio y alto
> se deja ver en día de fiesta,
> y abajo aguas azules
> con los reflejos de la luz blanquean . . . (AP, 293)

> . . . [Se sabe] lo que dice la tierra a la semilla
> y la semilla al viento . . . (AP, 246)

The sense of oneness with the cosmos is perhaps most eloquently encapsulated in the introductory verse of the poem «Seguro amor» (AP, 336): «Besar la flor es ya besar el mundo.» The poet's personal link to this universe is expressed epigrammatically in «Palabra Poética» (AP, 225) and is magnified by the use of the possessive: «Universo mío, vasto y humilde como el grano de arena.»

By virtue of this harmony, the poet is pervious and receptive to nature's message and heeds the celestial melodies that emanate from a Divine source:

> . . .Y porque está de pie sabe el lenguaje
> que hablan el árbol y la estrella
> en el momento único
> bajo la luz que se resuelve en otro . . . (AP, 175)

> Ya señor, sé lo que dicen
> las estrellas de tu cielo;
> que sus puntas de diamante
> me lo vienen escribiendo . . . (AP, 257)

> . . . Y cómo gira el mundo fijo,
> y que música, Dios, en tus abismos . . .(AP, 260)

> . . . Con ella este sonido del silencio
> se percibe tan claro . . .
> y cómo sale de ella el vuelo
> rumoroso del árbol . . . (AP, 204)

The poet clearly equates the accessibility of nature, its beauty and beneficent influence, with inner harmony. Thus does he apostrophize the passing cloud in the final verses of «La nube» (AP, 126), desirous of permanently holding its beauty within him: «. . . Déjame tu color, alza tu sueño/ y clava tu belleza en mi camino.»

A natural corollary of love of nature is the fear of debarment from her living images. In «Conversación a mi padre» (AP, 234) separation from nature through death is, for the poet, «lo de menos.» It is the loss of natue in his lifetime that inspires greater fear:

> . . .Lo de más será que nos quedamos ciegos o deformes
> y no podamos ver un día la luz del sol
> ni tomar en los dedos una rosa
> porque los ojos estén caídos en un pozo de nieblas
> y los dedos se nos hayan quedado secos como la estopa . . .

Again, in «Viejos versos de hoy» (AP, 96) and «El miedo» (DTA, 25) it is the loss of visual contact with nature that the poet most laments: «Este sentir que la vida se acaba/ y ya no ver más que niebla en redor. . . . Todo al diablo, sin mi cielo.»

Disharmony can be righted by the spirit and wisdom of the cosmos. In the poem «Paz perdida» (AP, 289) the poet's search for a lost harmony is largely undertaken admist natural elements:

> Te he buscado . . .
> . . . en el alma del cielo.
> Te he buscado en vigilia,
> y en lo hondo del sueño;
> y en el río que pasa
> y en los aires del viento . . .

The lonely traveler of the poem «El caminante» (AP, 337), engulfed in his despairing solitude, does not register nature's signs («. . . sin mirar . . . ni las estrellas»). Renewal of hope, at the poem's end, is linked with a restoration to him of nature: «. . . miró la luz que aparecía trémula/ de su salir al filo de la noche,/ y se alzó como un árbol en abril/ con el hábito ya de su esperanza.» In «En Bay Front Park» (AP, 285) and «Pensamientos en un día de sol» (AP, 315), the poet can shed his despairing self when he allows himself to be infused with nature's calming influence. In the first of these, a oneness with nature allows him to recenter himself:

> Aquí ya es otra cosa
> Ese vaho de muerte cotidiana,
> ese viento de rota mariposa,
>
> quedaron a mis pies, ya desprendidos
> de polvo, y fango y de veneno.
> Ahora ya está un sinfín de altos sonidos.
>
> Y un sol ardiente
> --limpio de negra voz endurecida--
> quema la escoria del dolor presente.
>
> Aquí está ya la maravilla
> de sentirse canción, y pensamiento,
> y gota de agua y tímida semilla.

The burden of death-giving images of the first stanzas («muerte,» «rota,» «polvo,» «fango,» «veneno») begins to be lifted in the third stanza as a beneficent nature cleanses and restores. The force of the thrice repeated «Aquí ya . . . Ahora ya . . . Aquí está» gains momentum and the poem's visual field moves from the lowest recesses («quedaron a mis pies») to the lift of renewed hope and harmony within nature's sphere: «Aquí está ya la maravilla/ de sentirse canción y pensamiento,/ y gota de agua, y tímida semilla.»

In «Pensamientos en un día de sol,» a line of demarcation between city and country living is clearly drawn. If the one invites a litany of horrors, nature inspires from the poet a hymn of praise, restoring to him his composure and renewed gratitude for its blessings. The negative images of the poem's first part (sixteen verses), always prefaced by «Es cierto que hay . . . cierto sí, cierto sí, cierto que») are forcefully offset in the poem's second part as the poet moves from the realities of city life to an appreciation of nature which, in turn, leads into a final Deo gratia:

> *. . . Cierto que . . . sí; pero a pesar de todo,*
> *pero como la luz cae desde Dios,*
> *y hace lo verde de las hojas nuevas,*
> *y el azul de la fuente, o el del mar,*
> *y el amarillo puro de la flor . . .*
> *como que nos conformamos con todo lo demás,*
> *y, en fin, que damos gracias a Dios*
> *porque este mayo nos ha dejado ver otra vez la primavera*

Even when far from its precincts the poet, through evocation of nature, is revivified and restored:

> *La única presencia*
> *la que reduce el mundo al centro*
> *de nuestro ser.*
> *Aquélla, ésta de hoy,*
> *que puede ser de siempre;*
> *la que una vez fue y se repite*
> *ahora, llena de voz suave*
> *sobre una tierra seca. . . .*
> *Aun el ruido del mar, ya tan lejano,*
> *parece resonar cerca, trayendo*
> *con él lo ya perdido*
> *que recupera su presencia*
> *al escucharse una palabra dicha*
> *con sorprendente claridad.*
>
> *El mundo, pues, se reconoce*
> *en la luz de los ojos.*
> *Y ya todo está bien, todo afirmado*
> *en la cálida sangre verdadera.* (Presencia,» AP, 352)

At one with nature, the poet finds his true north: «. . . de qué esquina del cerebro me ha salido este deseo/ de decir que estoy contento,/ porque el cielo es azul . . .» (AP, 271).   It is within nature's benevolent realm that with Wordsworth(3) he can say:

> *With deep devotion, nature did I feel*
> *In that enormous city's turbulent world*
> *of men and things, what benefit I owed*
> *to Thee, and those domains of rural peace*

Where to the sense of beauty, first my heart
was opened.

Eros as the Tendance of the Soul

In Socratic and Christian thought, by virtue of the divine in him, man aspires to the good above time and mutability. The «right» life is the process by which the merely secular self is remade in the likeness of the eternal. Equally, when seen through an existential perspective, the ethical man undertakes the wholesale reconstruction of his nature in the light of his duty and the power of his freedom and chooses himself, not in his immediacy, but in his eternal validity. This triple perspective informs Florit's vision of Eros when it is understood as the tendance of the soul.

In polar opposition to Eros as the tendance of the body, already studied in an earlier chapter, this form of love sets no store on gratification of physical appetites. Instead it is an *amor ascendens,* a desirous going forth of the soul in quest of a union with its true good which is above it. In the language of religion, it is the narration of the pilgrimage of the soul on the way of salvation from the initial moment at which it feels the need of salvation to the final consummation.

As a follower of Eros, Florit travels on a dialectical way from that which is purely mutable to that which is absolutely immutable. The decreasing materialization and the increasing spiritualization mark the approximation to the divine, the spiritual, and the transcendent.(4) The concept of a radical opposition of the body, representing the multiplicity of passion, and the soul, representing the intellect, and the description of the soul's journey conform closely, in Florit's poetry, to Greek and Christian thought: the journey is recognizably the same: the travel of the soul from temporality to eternity.

The Life of Thought

In his pursuit of knowledge, the philosopher-poet strives to make his soul as independent as he can from the fortunes of the body. For, the body with its wants and passions, its pleasures and pain, is a hindrance to the apprehension of reality and interferes with the prosecution of truth. Marked by «temperance» (control over physical appetites), the poet trusts to thinking rather than to sense. Whether his search is understood existentially as the pursuit of self-direction based on self-knowledge, or platonically as the pursuit of eternal wisdom or mystically as the pursuit of salvation, it is incumbent on the poet-philosopher to achieve and exercise rationality. Hence, the unremitting preoccupation with thinking as a philosophic form of purgation. It is through the life of thought, exalted repeatedly by Florit in other contexts, that intelligence may be progressively purified from any alien elements and win spiritual independence.

The hunger for wisdom is not easily satisfied. The poet as philosopher (aspirant after wisdom), of whom Eros is the chief, feels hunger for wisdom, the fairest of things, precisely because it remains unsatisfied. His whole life is a struggle with many an alternation of success and failure. The poem «Homenaje a Quevedo» (DTA, 63) makes clear the contradictory nature of Eros («entre mi pensamiento y mi deseo») and the weight of man's burden («cargado voy de mí y enamorado»). Even where the soul leaves behind prior stations of desire, a struggle must be waged to subdue and purify thought: «Verdad y belleza: qué difíciles y qué necesarias!» (AP, 225). If Florit is faithful to the Socratic principle that human life must be dictated by intelligence to be valuable, such intelligence involves self-knowledge and a correct estimate of what things have intrinsic what merely instrumental value. Through the exercise of the intellect, the perception of Platonic essences is made possible: «Con el aire dormido se pasea/ en una eternidad de pensamientos;/ libre su esencia por la idea/ y el ala libre por los vientos» (AP, 185).

In «El ciego» (DTA, 37), positioning himself and the reader in the arena of his own inwardness, Florit gives us the quintessential expression of an *amor ascendens* which draws on thought rather than sense in its perception of «good» or «reality.» Recalling man to the divine imperatives and to the condition of faith, the poet eclipses material reality («con los ojos cerrados»), strives to achieve a rationality with which he is not naturally endowed and must struggle to attain («abrir de par en par el pensamiento . . .

y si el pensar nos duele como flechas») and moves from a state of darkness («esta oscuridad de ciego . . . en mi noche») into the light of attainment («cómo entran las luces»). In this ascent to knowledge, the poet is able momentarily to put off temporality and put on eternity:

> Estar así, con los ojos cerrados,
> y abrir de par en par el pensamiento.
> ¿Cómo entran las luces
> en esta oscuridad de ciego?
> ¿Cómo decir lo que nos pasa
> si todo lo de fuera ya es silencio?
> Y si el pensar nos duele como flechas,
> ¿cómo dejar de ser, si estamos siendo?
> Si estamos siendo con los ojos ciegos,
> siendo más, por sentir que nos envuelve
> aire mas verdadero.
> Lo de fuera está allí.   Mas en mi noche
> Lo más es lo de dentro.
> ¿Un segundo? ¿Un minuto?   Lo que fuere.
> Apenas un latido de mi tiempo.
> Con los ojos cerrados
> Ya se tiene noticia de lo eterno.

The dichotimization of Eros as the tendance of the body and the tendance of the soul, and the role of thought in the process of moral development is clearly posited in «Seguro amor» (AP, 336). Here, the flower stands as a double metaphor of mutable form and permanent essence. The triumph of thought over passion, in the process of purification, is conveyed through color imagery: «Amor que frente al rojo se recrea/ como más tarde gozará del blanco/ porque sabe que amar es más seguro/ cuando más lo pensamos.»

The intellectual part of the soul is akin to the divine and is capable, through purification, of contact with its principle. When the soul turns to the world of intelligible forms it can soar to spiritual heights:

> Tan alto como tú, árbol que asomas
> en esta luz violeta de la tarde,
> el pensamiento solo está, temblando

callado como tú, en el alma sola. (AP, 181, #3)

> *... Estás aquí, por el ocaso herida,*
> *más alta que la flor del pensamiento...* (AP, 286)

In self-possession and prepossession («Aquí está ya la maravilla/ de sentirse canción y pensamiento,» AP, 285) the poet may encounter beauty through the exercise of reason («. . . por el pensamiento,/ vayamos todos, cada uno a su modo/ embelleciendo un poco nuestro rincón de vida,» AP, 316). In an existential sense, human choice and self-commitment can actually create human nature and determine a world of fact and value.

Yet, unlike the existentialists who awaken to meaning without the support or mediation of God, man, or nature, Florit looks, in a body of poems, toward a source of evaluation beyond himself, thereby ratifying the belief held by Martin Buber that «The encounter with the original voice, the original source of yes or no, cannot be replaced by any self-encounter.»(5) Intellectual serenity feeds directly into spiritual serenity. In the poem «El alto gris» (AP, 212), through the poet's «fervoroso pensamiento,» the soul is freed from the terrestrial «aquí» to set forth in its ascent to a supercelestial space of pure form, and to an encounter with its source:

> *Que está más alto Dios lo sabes*
> *tú por el fervoroso pensamiento.*
> *Aquí, vacío de palabras*
> *y casi ya vacío de recuerdos.*
>
> *Alma de paz que al cielo de la tarde*
> *subes en brazos del silencio*
> *cuando se asoma débil entre nubes*
> *un sol amarillento.*

The poems «Versos» (AP, 240) and «Lo de siempre» (AP, 246) incarnate man's hunger for a wisdom that will afford him an apprehension of ontological truths. The leit-motif of the first poem, «como no sabes,» stands in direct contraposition to that of the second, «se sabe,» as if to suggest the tension that inheres in man's quest. In «Versos,» the struggle for knowledge, posited in terms of human inadequacy («no sabes»), is played out in a time-space continuum with a decisive accent on flux. The first, second, and third stanzas, for example, are centered consecutively on «night,» «day,» and «the flower,» all metaphors of time's flow. This emphasis, moreover, is heightened by having the natural stress of the first verse of stanzas one, two, and four fall on the key verb «pasar» («como no sabes lo que pasa») with an alternative stress, in stanza three, on man's ignominious ignorance (y como, pues, no sabes»). The progression toward permanence («lo que queda») can only be made by moving from a consideration of sensible forms to those which are intelligible. «Night,» «day,» «the flower,» the plethora of colors of stanza five («¿será blanco y azul como este libro,/ o rojo y púrpura como el ocaso,/ o amarillo y rosado de la aurora,/ verde tal vez como este mar»), mutable forms all, are lost in the passage to a divine and immutable realm, described in stanza six. The intense visual impact of the sensible world is replaced by the soothing grayness («Dios gris») of the eternal godhead. Not in and of the flux, it is given to God alone to «pensar lo permanente» and, in direct opposition to mortal man, «mirar lo que nos queda.» While man cognizes the futility of his quest («. . . Pero es que ni tú, ni yo, ni aquél/ ni nadie, ni cualquiera,/ sabemos lo que pasa o lo que queda») he is yet impelled to undertake it.

«Lo de siempre,» per contra, while seconding man's search for effective knowledge of his circumstance and causation, stresses first what certitude man holds:

> Se sabe que la lluvia
> baja como los ángeles del cielo . . .
> Se sabe que soñamos
> cada noche que pasa mucho menos . . .
> También se sabe mucho
> de por qué nos movemos
> y de por qué besamos
> y pensamos con el pensamiento . . .
> Se sabe lo que mueve
> los mares y los pechos,
> lo que dice la tiera a la semilla
> y la semilla al viento . . .

Yet, the poet moves swiftly to reveal that the unquestioning assumptions of man are ineffectually shallow where fundamental questions of causation are concerned: «. . . Acostumbrados todos/ a escuchar la canción, a oír el verso,/ ni preguntamos cómo se hacen/ ni de dónde vinieron. . . .» Destined in his earthly life to see without «seeing» and to know without «knowing,» man ultimately looks toward a higher form of being: «. . . Ya ves, Señor, qué pena/ la de saberlo todo sin saberlo./ Y más aún la pena de no verte,/ aunque sabemos que estás en el cielo.» While both «Versos» and «Lo de siempre» testify to man's failure to win supreme knowledge in his life, they nonetheless demonstrate how, through its pursuit, he readies himself for full fruition.

As seen, then, thought is the principal motor of *an amor ascendens* and is indispensable for communion. Yet, its work once done, it must be transfigured and clarified by faith.

Serenity Through Faith

For the poet racked on the contradiction of existence, Christianity offers in this world the new immediacy of life by grace and the hope of Paradise in the world beyond. Faith accepts uncertainty and transcends it in an act of assent, surrendering reason to the Mystery of Revelation. God is found to be the sole sufficient point of reference for human existence.

Shedding the complexities, the bleak, godless landscapes of his darkest hours, Florit presents us, instead, with a benevolent Creator whose presence is inferred from his creation. In «Canto del mar» (AP, 190) and «Que estás en los cielos» (AP, 223), to cite two examples, nature is clearly perceived as the ground of that creativity which pervades it:

> *Para llegar hasta el rincón más hondo de la sangre*
> *tu canto, mar, viene en azul palabra y blanca risa*
> *dentro de la perfecta soledad de las horas.*
>
> *Dios está aquí. Más que en la cárcel de los templos,*
> *aún más que en el triángulo y en la lengua de fuego,*
> *Dios, el de la belleza, está aquí, vigilante . . .*
>
> («Canto del mar»)

Te he visto muchas veces.
Sí, pero aquella noche . . .

Te vi la tarde de la tempestad,
con látigo de fuego,
con agua despeñada de lo alto
y en nubes de carrera loca.

Te vi otra tarde, azul,
caído entre los árboles
a florecer como una luz de luna
entre el verde con frío del arroyo.

Sí, pero aquella noche . . .

Te he visto siempre donde la belleza:
muerte herida del sol,
alba rosada de ángel y de alondra,
y en la risa y el llanto verdaderos . . .

(«Que estás en los cielos»)

Similarly, the sanctity and divine significance of external objects is understood by the poet in «Nocturno III» (AP, 117) as he strives to be at one («sentir,» «ser,» «ver») with this natural reality and its purpose:

Dime qué puedo hacer para sentir sobre mis sienes
tu hueco de jazmines en el agua
y esa oculta semilla que cruza en alas de los astros.

Dime qué palpitar me falta
para ser como el canto de tus noches,
noche desde que ayer se estremecieron.

Sí, sí: dime la fronda de tus árboles
y la pequeña nube perdida detrás del rastro de la luna.

Me dirás tu color --ciego de mí, que no lo veo--,
tu forma de naranja desleída
y tu acento callado por el aire
cuando caen al mar los fríos ataúdes de tus muertos.

The interfusion of God and nature is also implicit in «Versos» (AP, 240) where the «coloration» of the Creator is sought in a natural realm: «. . . será . . . o rojo y púrpura como el ocaso,/ o amarillo y rosado de la aurora, verde tal vez como este mar,/ como la cinta, como son las hojas?» Or again, the designs and purposes of an immanent deity are sometimes revealed in celestial landscapes («Ya, señor, sé lo que dicen/ las estrellas de tu cielo,» AP, 257), in visions of an orderly, stable universe («. . . y cómo gira el mundo fijo,» AP, 259) and in the perception of a cosmic harmony taken in a conative rather than an epistemological sense («. . . mundos/ que no se ven, pero que suenan tímidos/ como un abrir de flor . . . y qué música, Dios, en tus abismos,» AP, 259).

Yet Florit's God is not in and of the world alone, and also represents a divine order. The poet's religious consciousness attributes predicates to the transcendental God that are symbolic in character. While temporal links between God and the world are established, his primary relation appears to be a spatial one. In «Radioastronomía» (AP, 259), for example, God is essentially depicted as outside the spherical universe, though a possible intersection of a divine order and a time order is suggested in the description of the milky way:

> *Y alto sobre su giro*
> *de luz lechosa va el Camino*
> *dando su vuelta al infinito*
> *cada vez más atroz, hundido*
> *como un puñal en el centro de Dios mismo . . .*

Equally, in «Asonante final» (AP, 266), God stands outside the parameters of the firmament: «. . . Dios, que parece dormir/ en esta tarde al otro lado/ de su cielo de azules imposibles. . . .» While the spatial positioning of God «above» earth may be enriched with secondary symbolic meaning, other poems suggest, rather, a candorous acceptance of the lessons of catechism which depict a God literally dwelling in a heaven above: «. . . Sabemos que estás en el cielo» (AP, 247). «. . . Que estás en los cielos» (AP, 223). «. . .Dios, que está en los cielos . . .» (AP, 255).

As described by Florit in «Asonante final,» for example, this God is a familiar, quasi anthropomorphic figure, and the poet's faith, here, has to be understood contextually as an

expression of a culture phenomenon, a folk-religion, a second
nature for all those who are born in Christiandom:

> *. . . ¿Sabes, Señor, lo que pensaba*
> *mientras que me estaba afeitando?*
> *Pues en que todos nosotros,*
> *los españoles y los hispanoamericanos*
> *tenemos tanta confianza contigo,*
> *porque como tantas veces te nombramos,*
> *a cada una de ellas te vamos creando. . .*
> *y por eso hasta tí llegamos*
> *en traje de casa, sin aspavientos,*
> *a veces casi malcriados . . .*

Yet, while the God of «Asonante final» is whittled down to human
dimensions, Florit clearly cognizes His infinite qualitative difference from man.   Thus, the realization that all he is and does
is a divine gratuity is given devotional expression in a series of
Deo Gratia: «. . . damos gracias a Dios, porque este mayo nos
ha dejado ver otra vez la primavera» (AP, 316).   «. . .Y dar gracias
a Dios por el día y la noche/ y por tener una palabra nuestra aquí,
en donde nadie nos/ conoce» (AP, 314).   «. . . Dios mío, gracias
por haberme dado/ la máquina y los dedos,/ y la hoja de papel,/
y las palabras en que se abre el pensamiento./   Gracias por
dejarme estar, dejarme ser . . .» (AP, 272). «gracias, gracias,/
por la pluma y el papel/ y más por el amor de ver la noche/ y
de sentir que Dios, que está en los cielos,/ está dentro de mí
también» (AP, 255).   «. . . pobre hombre solo,/ triste de soledades cuando anochece,/ Mas a pesar de todo agradecido/ por
lo que Dios me da de pan y lecho/ de amistad y familia . . .»
(AP, 342).
   Because in the light of faith self-causation or self-creation is
reserved for God alone, the most fitting attitude for finite man
is that of enlightened acquiescence to the divine plan that governs
his life and his death.   The filial submission to God's will in
Florit's poetry is reminiscent of the Loyolan third grade of humility
as these verses of «Agua lejana» (AP, 243) reveal: «. . . Como
luego, más tarde/ como algún día/ he de mirar la muerte/ cuando
Dios diga.» Again, in «Variaciones sobre un verso de fray
Diego de Hojeda» (AP, 338), after postulating his desire for union

with God, Florit concludes the poem on a note of acceptance: «. . . Y así, pues hay que ser, he de rendirme/ a ser como tú quieras:/ hombre tenaz que siente el mayor vuelo/ y se afirma a la tierra.»

Trust and faith in a paternal God, innocent, here, of all inquisition or conjecture, embolden the poet with eschatological surety:

> . . . Por eso cuando tú nos dices
> que se acabó este juego de aquí abajo,
> vamos a tu cielo, los que vayamos,
> con la tranquilidad de quien después de un paseo
> vuelve a ver a su padre que le estaba esperando,
> y que le dice, buenas noches, hijo . . . (AP, 273)

In «Conversación a mi padre» (AP, 234), the death of the poet's father is not marked by sorrow but instead is accepted with a simple and unswerving belief in a continued existence beyond the grave which replicates all the happy things and experiences of life. His father, visualized in a happy heaven «above,» knows a bliss, which is different in degree but not in kind from the happy existence of earthy life:

> . . . Tu bien estás, creo yo, allá arriba.
> ¿Fuiste por fin a tu tierra de Castilla,
> como pensé que harías?
> De seguro que te habrá gustado
> encontrarte con tantas gentes amigas
> y ponerte con ellas a conversar
> en una era de Cubas al mediodía . . .

No longer the feared adversary of the poet's despairing hours, death, here, is viewed as «una generosa caricia» (AP, 134), the entrance to a better state.

The Dying Life: The Via Purgativa

The faith that enables the poet to face death with equanimity suggests the certification by him of the principle that in death the

soul effects its release of the body, thereby rising above mutability. This «release» and the concomitant participation of the
soul in the supreme good, whether viewed through the prism of
Hellenic or mystic thought, cannot be won in this life. Yet, this
life can be well used if it is directed to preparation for full fruition
of the eternal good beyond the limits of temporal existence.
Therefore, in both Hellenic and Christian writings, the highest life
for man while he is on earth is a «dying life» aimed at furthering,
as far as it can, the soul's independence of the body: «. . .
¿Cuándo, fray Luis, será que pueda/ alzarme sobre el cieno,
desafiándote,/ carne mortal; vencerte, pensamiento;/ romper lo
que me ata, lo que duele . . .» (DTA, 57). The conversion toward
God, then, is essentially a process of purification, moral
perfecting, and development.

Florit concurs with the Platonic belief that man is not meant to
dwell in the cave. Rather, he is naturally called upon to ascend
from a lower to a higher order. The soul's dream of perfection
is understood «essentially» by Florit and forms part of a natural
design:

> El ave alta sobre el mar.
> Alta la nube por el cielo.
> La canción en el aire, alta.
> Y el alma alta por su sueño . . .(AP, 183)

> . . . como el alma, la alondra
> sube y sube a los cielos. (AP, 256)

Yet, participation in the true good is implemented «existentially»
and is not won without battle. Man's life is put into his charge
to commit and dispose; the dialectic soul evaluates itself in its
struggle to have what is best in its nature rule over what is worse.

The language of spiritual progress in Florit's poetry involves
journeys, voyages, ascents, and nocturnal landscapes. Several
such symbols are used effectively in «Canción del nocturno»
(DA, 66) and «El otro ardor» (AP, 264). In the first of these,
the poet's struggle for perfection is enacted in an oneiric setting
(«en oasis de sueños») which promotes the stripping bare of those
wordly layers that tend to conceal and obscure the essential
self:

> Corazón de mis noches

> *desnudo de palabras,*
> *hecho sobre las ascuas*
> *de recuerdos y goces . . .*
> *(Saber que voy desnudo*
> *bajo miles de estrellas . . .*

Water imagery equally conforms to directional symbols of progress conveying the idea of movement from the material to the spiritual (and ultimately from the finite to the infinite):

> *. . . Navego por las horas*
> *que más sufren el frío*
> *de un paisaje vivido*
> *más allá de estas cosas.*

> *(Huir en la corriente*
> *por la mitad del alma,*
> *que se acerca en la blanca*
> *inquietud de esta muerte.) . . .*

Yet, the recurring use of disquieting imagery clearly suggests the difficulty of the journey and the pull of opposing impulses: «. . . Hundido en el desierto/ de arenas indecisas . . . el frío/ de un paisaje . . . Qué ríos . . . de frías aguas tímidas . . . la blanca inquietud de esta muerte . . . .»

A battle between a higher and a lower order is also suggested in «El otro ardor.» Again, the material of the poem is the substance of a vision or «dream» wherein the soul effects an apparently effortless entry into a divine realm, soaring aloft into the vast empyrean: «No hay que volver. Que la aventura es esa:/ al cielo van el sueño y la saeta/ y por el cielo, ángeles y estrellas. . . .» Acquiescence to the divine plan is implied by water imagery whereby the river of living water flows, unimpeded, to the vast sea of eternal being: «. . . Velas del sino sobre el mar. Destino/ de seguir a los vientos en su giro/ por bajar con las aguas de los ríos/ hasta dar en la vida. . . .» In his «dream,» the entrance to a *via unitiva* is already sighted as the poet envisions a movement from reason to rapture (the «ardor» of the poem's title):

> *. . . de manera*

que sin dejar de ser todo se vuelva
como junto a la luz queda la cera.

Y entonces, al pisar los altos suelos,
como que ya no pesa el pensamiento,
se como flota, como vuela ardiendo . . .

Yet, the *prima facie* evidence of serenity is suddenly dispelled with the penultimate stanza. Here, the poet «awakens» from his dream of attainment and is thrust back upon a *via purgativa* and the internal struggle between *sic* and *non* that it implies: «. . . Y cómo al fin del sueño se apodera/ un liviano quehacer --la ligereza/ del otro ardor, de la tortura inmensa/ de no querer lo que queremos. . . .»

«Viejos versos de hoy» (AP, 96) stands, perhaps, as the quintessential expression of the concept of purification as the «dying life.» In consonance with the soul's anticipated independence of the body, life becomes a long rehearsal for dying and involves the rejection of terrestrial bonds, the putting off of the old man with the affections and lusts («. . . la mirada lasciva . . .cada impulso venal») and the creation of a «new» self. The repeated allusions to death in the poem, then, must be understood symbolically within the context of the desired emancipation from an earthly bondage, hence as an approximation to a «dying life.» That readiness is effected through the deliberate exercise of the will is made clear as the poet feels, conceptualizes, and calibrates his own progress: «Este sentir que la vida se acaba. . . . Por el correr de la vida que acaba/ se entra a mirar cómo viene el morir/ y ya vivir es un sueño sin forma,/ lejos del ser, en la noche sin fin. . . .» Disengagement from life is linked, once more, to a water union: «. . . Viene al morir con un gusto divino/ para morder el sabor de la mar.» Yet, while the poet's goal is clearly articulated, it is the reality of the struggle that finally asserts itself in the corpus of the poem. Beginning with the antithesis of the poem's title, «Viejos versos de hoy,» the recurring engagement of opposing forces, yesterday as today, today as tomorrow, is implied. At the same time that the writer's progress is being posited, it is also being countered by opposing recollections still etched in the poet's psyche. Thus, the night and sea of purgation are offset by their opposite numbers: «. . . Cuánto llorar por el *suelo*, abatido,/ bajo el calor de las lenguas del *sol.*»

The poet's present «gozo» does not eclipse the remembrance of sorrow («Alza el dolor su mirada»), nor does the thrice repeated «ya» of spiritual purification («. . . ya no ver más que nieblas en redor . . . ya vivir en un sueño sin forma. . . . Ya para ahogar la mirada lasciva . . .») diminish the recall of a prior state («. . . Lúbrico ayer con las manos trementes/ a cada alzar de una cálida voz . . .») or the impact of continued temptation («. . . Ya para ahogar la mirada lasciva,/ muere al nacer cada impulso venal . . .»). Finally, the repeated use of gustatory images to signal the poet's realization of a «dying life» suggests, through the presence of vestigial sensorial responses, that, in fact, he has fallen short of his goal. This conclusion appears to be validated by the mixed images of the final verse («. . . para morder el sabor de la mar. . .») given the impossibility of a satisfactory setting of «teeth» to «water»: «. . . Gozo de estar paladeando la muerte/ para beber una gota de Dios. . . . Viene el morir con un gusto divino/ para morder el sabor de la mar.»

Therefore, despite sincere commitment to self-discipline, the poet's *via purgativa* does not carry him along an unbroken path. He falters--then rallies, constrained to mold again and again in decision and action, the integrity of a goal at once actual and ideal.

The poem «La única» (AP, 130), records for us, once again, in microcosm, the nature of this process. The resolve to live a «dying life» again flows from the view of death as deliverance and as entrance to a better state. The poet begins with an ineffable sense of the wonder, beauty, and glory of the Ultimately Real which he is beckoned to view by Death, personified as «la única» of the poem's title. Believing the vision of the Ultimate to be within his reach, he models his life on the reality of Death: «Allí, yo sí la siento/ porque está donde el sol, brillante, y pura;/ en el punto feliz riendo, llamándome/ con el abrazo abierto siempre. . . .» The poet's determination to heed this call is translated, principally, into images of space and time for, despite the «otherness» of his vision, he nonetheless still moves in a time-space continuum.

The locus of the divine realm of «La única,» with its distance or nearness to the poet serving as signposts of progress or slack, acts as one of the poem's central foci. In the first stanza, it is enough for him to intuit the locus of this realm: «Allí yo sí la siento/ porque está donde el sol, brillante y pura; en el punto feliz. . . .» In subsequent stanzas, however, metaphorical muscle is given to the concept of a *via purgativa* as a journey along a prescribed route leading from materialization to spiritualization through repeated use of spatial images: «. . . Y he de ir hacia ella/ cada día más cerca. . . .» In stanza three, the poet appears to suggest that while transcendent reality is present within the concrete world («. . . allí sí, en aquel punto callado de la tierra/ y allí donde cayó desprendida una estrella . . .»), the heavenly realm of «la única» stands outside the orbits of space and time and thereby remains invisible to mortal sight. Such a break-point is clearly inscribed in the following verses: «. . . Donde desaparecen en el mar los navíos;/ donde en el cielo desaparecen las palomas. . . .» While stanza four denotes appreciable advancement along the path of purification («. . . Qué cerca aquella noche . . .»), the jolting antithesis of the final stanza («. . . Y ahora otra vez en lejanía . . .») stresses how long and hard the way. The poet, fallen back on his path, must immerse himself in the struggle anew.

In and of the flux, the poet's is a journey in time as well as space. Gradations of failure or success in his trajectory, there-fore, are also marked by images of time. Intuition, expressed in a present tense («Allí yo sí la *siento* . . .») moves to resolve enacted in time («. . . Y *he de* ir hacia ella/ --*cada día* más cerca, más seguro»). Levels of complexity materialize through fluctuations in time («. . . Qué cerca *aquella noche . . . y ahora otra vez* . . .») yet despair at being grounded once more in the present is mitigated by the force of the adverbial «aún» («. . . que *aún* no son el sol brillante») with its implication of future promise. In direct contrast to the zigzagging process which engages mortal man, the poet suggests, by virtue of the unchanging attributes which he assigns to «la única,» that she represents an eternal realm. This is heightened by repetition («el sol, brillante y pura,» «. . . punto feliz,» «. . . punto callado,» «riendo,» «risa . . .»), the reiteration of the same verb («llamándome») and especially by the duplication of the last verses of stanzas one and five which, in their final exaltation of the adverb «siempre» clearly accentuate the immutable nature of this realm.

In addition to temporal and spatial images, the poem relies heavily on acoustical and visual effects. As outlined by Ewer in *A Survey of Mystic Symbols,* spiritual hearing expresses the conative side of cosmic harmony. First, the poet as addres-

129

see, receives and decodes the celestial message conveyed by acoustical impression: «. . . está . . . en el punto feliz *riendo, llamándome.* . . .» The steadfastness of this call is accentuated, as already noted, by the presence of the gerund «llamándome» in all of the poem's stanzas but one. The pilgrim's proximity to his goal (participation in a cosmic harmony) is measured musically as if to symbolize the impact of divine reality on the human soul («. . . cada día . . . más seguro/ de escuchar su canción. . . . Qué cerca aquella noche./ Un revuelo de notas . . .»).

Yet, if harmony is the most instructive of senses, vision is surely the most luminous. The dazzling brilliance of the final station on the pilgrim's way («está donde el sol, brillante y pura») suggests, on the one hand, that arrival at this locus involves conscious illumination. For, as the soul's superior principle acquires its natural place in the hierarchy of values, some light begins to shine on that objective darkness of material desire. This light can increase by irradiating («. . . cada día . . . más seguro . . . de ver») or decrease by darkening («. . . otra vez . . . el camino en los ocasos tristes») because of the freedom with which the soul is endowed. The poet's eventual arrival at his destination is therefore linked with the sun as a manifestation of and a participation in the divine. The radiance of eternity emanating from this light differs qualitatively from the commonplace «. . . luz de indiferentes soles/ que aún no son el sol brillante y puro. . . .» The vision of a «lumen gloriae» is, as always, coupled with darkness («Qué cerca aquella noche») as a reminder that only of darkness can the light be born. The substance of the poem, complemented by the poetic praxis, is the «vision» of something standing beyond, toward which in his conscious life he gropingly makes his way.

In two later poems, «El viaje» (AP, 295) and «El hombre solo» (AP, 342), in a spirit of continued testing of ideas and of self, the poet expresses cautious satisfaction at his progress along the purgative way. In the first, he is able to claim, «. . .Los años me florecen/ con más limpio mirar.» In the second, more analytical poem, he is cleansed of all «hubris» and comes to accept himself as he really is:

> *Que el aire del invierno me rodea*
> *para purificarme de mis sueños*
> *y así dejarme a lo que soy: un hombre*

> *solo y por desvalido, un alma seca*
> *al amor de la lumbre que se apaga,*
> *siempre esperando lo que nunca llega.*

In the first poem, the qualifier («más limpio») and in the second, the continued requirement of discipline («para purificarme de mis sueños») both speak to the fact that purification is not yet complete.

Yet, the penance, the self-discipline, the disengagement of the senses associated with the *via purgativa* facilitate the realization of a state of grace and, with it, the contemplation, meditation, and concentration of the soul in God.

The Via Illuminativa

The juncture of these two ways and passage from the first to the second is signaled in several poems by the resounding adverbial qualifier «ya» again suggesting a yoking of symbols of time and space in the poetic praxis. The long previous travail is therefore implicitly, sometimes metaphorically, recorded: «. . . Tan libre el alma ya de sus quisieras» (AF, 254); «. . . Ya sobre mí» (AP, 88); «. . . Ya no baja al cristal de mi poesía/ una gota de ardor, desde el venero/ de la nieve de ayer hoy sólo mía . . .» (AP, 134).

Arrival at a higher level in «Soneto,» #6 (AP, 87) does not preclude continued dialectical evaluation wherein lower levels and prior stations are recalled. The present «dying life,» for example, is contrasted with its opposite («Habréis de conocer que estuve vivo . . .»), vestiges of that anterior state remain («. . . una sombra que tendrá mi frente . . .») or are evoked in negative opposition to the present («. . . sin el ardor lascivo,/ sin el sueño. . . . Qué sueño sin ensueños torcedores. . . . Qué lejana la voz de los amores»). Indeed, at the very outset of the poem, the interfusion of distinct verbal tenses suggests a conscious journey in time (*italics mine*): *Habréis de* conocer que *estuve vivo*/ por una sombra que *tendrá* mi frente./ Sólo en mi frente la inquietud *presente*/ que hoy *guardo* en mí, de mi dolor cautivo.» The «inquietud presente» alluded to in the fourth verse may be understood metaphorically as a bondage to time:

while the poet has succeeded in realizing a «dying life» he is not
yet free of the fetters of the body.   Despite the sense of temporal
process, however, the final tercets are instrumental in bringing the
poem's center of gravity back to present illumination and to
the concomitant readiness to receive God:

> *Habréis de conocer que estuve vivo*
> *por una sombra que tendrá mi frente.*
> *Sólo en mi frente la inquietud presente*
> *que hoy guardo en mí, de mi dolor cautivo.*
>
> *Blanca la faz, sin el ardor lascivo,*
> *sin el sueño prendiéndose a la mente.*
> *Ya sobre mí, callado eternamente,*
> *la rosa de papel y el verde olivo.*
>
> *Qué sueño sin ensueños torcedores,*
> *abierta el alma a trémulas caricias*
> *y sobre el corazón fijas las manos.*
>
> *Qué lejana la voz de los amores.*
> *Con qué sabor la boca a las delicias*
> *de los altos serenos oceanos.*

A temporal perspective is equally central to the poem «Para
mañana» (AP, 77) which hinges on the interaction between the
three ec-stases of time. Here, the soul having been prepared
in a figurative yesterday of purgation («Como esta paz la tengo
tan sabida/ --son muchos años de mirarme el alma . . .») is, in
its present state, clearly divested of all material contingencies
(«. . . Presencia de una vida/ entre nieves intactas;/ puro cantar, . . . Amor, ya sin acento . . .»).   Various images suggest,
moreover, that with the realization of a «dying life» comes a
renascence in Christ.   Hence the «rosa de los veranos,» archtype
of ephemeral beauty, reflowers figuratively in the Lord («. . . en
íntimo capullo transformada . . .») much as divine love («. . . el
corazón abierto y la voz alta . . . Amor ya sin acento . . .») is born
of the ashes of material contingency.   Yet, the serenity of the
present is marred by the knowledge that the soul's freedom
cannot be fully realized in this life («. . . Sombra de estar la nube
detenida/ sobre un dolor sin lágrimas . . .»).   However, the

sorrow this causes is mitigated by acquiescence to a divine plan, hence the «dolor sin lágrimas» as the poet awaits the «sombra cierta/ que en los remansos de la tarde baja.» The poet, therefore, readies himself for a desired future («para mañana») and with it «el adiós eterno.» In the enactment of that final ritual, even the symbols that attach to a *via illuminativa* are swallowed signaling the erasure of all contingency: «. . . Adonde iré no irán conmigo/ ni rosa, ni dolor, ni amor, ni nada.»

When squarely positioned on the *via illuminativa,* the push and pull of opposing forces, associated with the *via purgativa,* are halted. Through the exercise of the will and the intellect, by virtue of his sentiment and cushioned by his faith, the poet makes ready to enter the dark night of the soul.

The Dark Night of the Soul

In a tone reminiscent of San Juan de la Cruz, Florit's readiness for the absolute negation of «night» wherein the soul «goes out of herself» to find herself again in God, is first formulated as a plea: «. . . Déjame morir de noche/ ya con la luz acabada,/ ya con la luz que me sirva/ para escaparme de casa . . .» (AP, 27). In «Canciones para la soledad» (AP, 182) and «Variaciones sobre un verso de Fray Diego de Hojeda» (AP, 338) the mystic way is suggested by chiaroscuro imagery wherein contingent light must be eclipsed for divine love to be experienced:

> . . . *Entre belleza con el sol venía*
> *dura y caliente por la luz de agosto.*
> *Nadie la vio pasar cerca del alma.* . . .
>
> *Cuando llegó en la noche de belleza*
> *--ala no más, ni acento, ni sonido--,*
> *ya el amor la tenía por el alma.*
>
> («Canciones para la soledad»)
>
> . . . *si el ojo para la mirada,*
> *dentro del fondo inmenso de lo oscuro*
> *descubre a Dios en la noche estrellada* . . .
>
> («Variaciones sobre un verso de

The correlation between night and the soul's readiness for God is again stressed in the concluding stanza of «Canción» (AP, 254) and is expressed as a *Deo gratia:* «. . . gracias . . . por el amor de ver la noche/ y de sentir.que Dios, que está en los cielos,/ está dentro de mí también.» It is, then, by the grace of God that the poet is enabled to «see» the night and, by extension, to sense the eternal Godhead in the darkness.

Yet, by antiphrasis, religion also seeks the light. In the *Phaedo* the soul on the verge of attainment is described as being about to lose herself in light, and the definition of God as light has necessitated the theological concept of the Beatific Vision. Certainly, Florit aspires to this light and if he cannot yet attain it, he reaches for it in a celestial sphere born of his own fervent imaginings: «. . . Y las luces empiezan a volver/ a donde las estrellas, no en lo alto,/ sino aquí para el cielo de juguete/ que imagina la sed . . .» (AP, 254). Apostrophizing «night,» the poet couples darkness with true light: «. . . Y en tus maravillosos ojos están las luces verdaderas/ que me abren un abismo de paz dentro del alma» (AP, 116). It is on that guiding light that the poet fixes his gaze, his idealism unabated, his inner vision unimpaired, his soul in peace and serenity: «Como esta paz la tengo tan sabida/ . . . no habrán de preguntarme, cuando llegue/ en qué luces prendía la mirada . . .» (AP, 77). As already noted, the poem «El ciego» (DTA, 37) shows that the divine light is not the object which the poet contemplates but the force which, entering his spirit, transforms it and renders it capable of seeing.

The human soul, being already free of the shadow of the sensible body, ardently desires to return to its true realm and to contemplate the ideal in a pure and luminous intuition. Clothed in the mystical language of desire and passion, the soul expresses its heart-hunger in «La noche» (AP 257) where a quasi-rapturous state is suggested by the alliterative babble of the concluding stanza («no sé. . .sí sé»):

> . . . *Y qué clara la escritura*
> *dentro de la noche, dentro*
> *del corazón anheloso*
> *de recibir este fuego*
>
> *que baja de tus abismos,*

va iluminando mi sueño
y mata la carne y deja
el alma en su puro hueso.

Lo que dicen las estrellas
me tiene, Señor, despierto
a más altas claridades,
a más disparados vuelos,

a un no sé de cauteloso,
a un sí sé de goce trémulo
(*alas de una mariposa*
agitadas por el suelo) . . .

With unconcealed ardor, the love-stricken soul expresses impatience and longing in «El resignado» (DTA), 57) and again borrows freely from a vocabulary of erotic love in «El ausente» (DTA, 39):

. . .¿Cuándo la noche eterna
ha de cubrir con sus estrellas de oro
este ardor, este sueño, este anhelar
que tienen acosada al alma sola? . . . («El resignado»)

. . . lo que espero con ansia. . . .
Un no sé qué de esperanza. . . .
Amor sin nombre se llama
lo que me tiene muriendo . . . («El ausente»)

Yet, in «15 de octubre de 1965» (AP, 345), the longing to escape from the phenomenal world and to rise into transcendent permanence is clothed both in a language of passion («. . . la pasión la misma . . .») and of restraint («. . . arde sin llama el hombre . . . la llama sin ardor que lo ilumina»). Restless yearnings are largely subdued and subordinated to calm acceptance («. . . y el constante anhelar sin desespero . . .»)

The apparent contradiction between ardor and restraint, urgency and resignation conforms to the paradoxical nature of religious experience which has been described by A. N. White-head as «something whose possession is the final good and yet is beyond all reach; something which is the ultimate ideal and the hopeless quest.»(6)   Christ stands as the ultimate personification of religious paradox.   As the Eternal-in-Time, the irruption of the Absolute into history, His is a «sign of contradiction.»(7) The cognition by Florit of the paradoxical nature of belief finds expression in several poems of religious theme («. . . más cerca de mi bien inalcanzable,» AP, 345; «. . . Un deseo de estar cerca de lo que miro tan lejos»; «. . . Amor sin nombre se llama,» DTA, 39).   As the essence of religion lies in experience rather than in intellectual belief, all attempts to logicize this paradox must perforce fail.   God stands on the «other side of being»; he may be apprehended but he cannot be comprehended by any of his creatures.

Instruments of Transcendence

The sudden jump or transference of consciousness to a transcendental realm is primarily portrayed by Florit in images of heavenward ascent.   The skylark of the poem «La tarde» (AP, 256), for example, is an emblematic representation of mortality in flight to transcendence («. . . Más alto, hacia arriba/ por caminos eternos,/ como el alma, la alondra/ sube y sube a los cielos»), and innumerable other examples can be adduced to illustrate how ecstatic gladness at contact with transcendent power is translated into images that lift, soar, and fly.

The poet may either passively receive these intimations from another world or he may actively seek and find within his own environment some image through which a transcendent reality can be conceived. Works of art, suggesting permanence, act not only as reliable analogues of transcendence but may also convey the impact of the vision of Beauty, Truth, and Goodness (held to be revelations of God) on the human soul.   Thus, it is on the «wings» of music in «A la música» (AP, 334) that the poet's spirit soars aloft and finds its way to the divine harmony of a transcendent realm:

> . . . eres tú el ala que nos guía. . . .
> Que tú, tú sola, con tus alas,
> eres constante compañía;
> la que puede llenar las horas,

más amada cuanto más mía;
la que me acerca más a Dios
cuando más lejos parecía.

Art again acts as the vehicle of transcendence in «El otro ardor»
(AP, 264) whereby the struggle between body and soul, between
a human and divine «ardor» is resolved.   The force of art on the
human soul and the final freeing of the spirit for flight is conveyed
in intense reaction to what is mortal:

> *. . . Y cómo al fin del sueño se apodera*
> *un liviano quehacer--la ligereza*
> *del otro ardor, de la tortura inmensa*
>
> *de no querer lo que queremos, hasta*
> *que por el arte nos abrasa y alza*
> *y de un tirón nos arrebata el alma.*

Silence is the metaphorical instrument facilitating the soul's
upward lift in «El alto gris» (AP, 212).   The intuition of a divine
realm «above» («Que está más alto Dios lo sabes») is offset by the
poet's «aquí» signaling his roots in a mutable realm where he is
but «un hilo de humo.»   Though the notion of God begins
abstractly («el fervoroso pensamiento»), it is soon transmuted by
the soul's hunger («con el amor dormido dentro») into a truth
more persuasive than the poet's own palpable reality («Más
firme,/ más verdadero/ que tú mismo»).   The soul in a state of
grace, free of all worldly sin, of that language which obstructs
the transmission and reception of the divine message («. . . vacío
de palabras/ y casi ya vacío de recuerdos. . .») surrenders to
silence and is uplifted to God: «. . . Tú lo sabes.   Que Dios/ abre
su rosa de invisible fuego/ ahora cuando, reina de la altura,/ sube
tu alma en brazos de silencio.»

The poet's solitude stands as a principal vehicle of
transcendence.   Bearing no resemblance to the solitude of alienation already studied, this aloneness represents a desired
and desirable state and one that is deliberately cultivated and
nurtured.   Its direct link with transcendence is established in
various poems and, more directly, in the lecture «Unas notas
sobre la soledad» prepared by Florit as an introduction to the
collection «Canciones para la soledad: «Puede el hombre, así,

como poeta, vivir entre los hombres. Pero es a condición de que sepa guardar su soledad para sus horas trascendentales.» In the body of the lecture, the writer draws a distinction between that solitude determined solely by physical apartness, and a solitude mandated by the requirements of the soul and which can be experienced anywhere: «Hay la soledad de quien, para estar solo, necesita no ver a nadie, huir de las gentes. Como la devoción del que para hablar con su Dios ha de entrar en el templo. Y hay la otra soledad. La que no se deshace con la risa y el canto. La que vive entre calles y plazas y multitudes.» In the first of these, there is the risk of self-indulgence whereby aloneness becomes an escape from the demands and duties of existence: «El poeta . . . no debe ser, como hombre, un sordo a los ecos del mundo. Han de dolerle a él todos los dolores de la humanidad.» In exalting the second type of solitude instead, «Esa heroica soledad que va con nosotros o que nosotros encontramos siempre que queremos buscarla,» Florit appears to echo the Emersonian credo that «It is easy in the world to live after the world's opinion; it is easy in solitude to live after our own, but the great man is he who in the midst of crowds keeps with perfect sweetness the independence of solitude.»(8) In «Homenaje a Quevedo» (DTA, 63) Florit formulates similar thoughts in words borrowed from the Baroque master: «. . . Por los claustros del alma/ podré estar apartado, mas no ausente;/ en soledad estoy, pero no solo;/ que sé bien estar solo entre la gente. . . .» There must be a dual contact with God and man, a moving easily and regularly from one to the other, making them to be a unity of experience. Yet this is a difficult accomplishment. Florit's «heroica soledad,» encountered among the «multitudes» becomes a compound metaphor of the mystic way: it is sought through purgation and illumination («. . . la soledad que vamos alimentando con nuestro alto pensamiento noble. . . . Y que de nuestra alma se alimenta y no la agota, sino que por milagro, ambos crecen a la par y a la par se elevan»); the determination, the strength, the self-denial, the elusiveness of the goal--are all part of the pain of the poet's *via crucis* («Duele, a veces . . . como una espina la soledad. . . . Duele como el silencio. Con qué fuertes brazadas hay que nadar hacia ella, que se nos escapa, que huye de nosotros. . . . Es un dolor que llena días y noches; que nos hace pensar en la inutilidad del esfuerzo por apresarla; es un dolor que nos tienta a abandonar el ímpetu»). Yet, the poet rallies and resolves to undertake the final lap («No dejes que se te escape.   Abrázala, aunque te duela, muy hondo, el abrazo.   Ella, por fin, se volverá compasiva, y te dará el calor suave del plumón de los cisnes»).   That solitude is directly instrumental in effecting an ineffable union with God is made clear at the article's conclusion.   Images of light, beauty, flight, and truth point unequivocally to contact with a numinous force and to a sudden visitation of transcendence: «Y pienso, también, que la soledad del poeta es dulce.   Que después de su lucha por entrar en ella, encuentra al fin, cuando rasga su velo, un haz iluminado en el que ve, con el alma transida de belleza, cómo bailan los átomos del aire y cómo los recuerdos que había olvidado vuelven a aletear, ya libre de su escoria, por el espacio del sueño.»

The link between solitude and transcendence is again established in «Canciones para la soledad,» #19 (AP, 185).   The stages of the soul's preparation for union are alluded to, *grosso modo,* and move from intuition of the divine light, to desire of God and, implicitly, through the aforementioned phase of solitude, to union with the Beloved (the mystical «navegar» of the soul):

> *Hacia la luz tenía el alma*
> *¡y era tan poco!*
>
> *Hacia el amor volaba el alma*
> *¡y era tan poco!*
>
> *Hacia la soledad navega el alma*
> *¡y ahora sí es todo!*

The conversion of the sorrow of solitude-sought into the sweetness of solitude-found is again suggested in poem #4 (181) of the same collection:

> *¡Qué dulce ya con ella*
> *mientras la tarde baja*
> *y se van encendiendo*
> *las estrellas del alma!*

The most eloquent equation of solitude-transcendence, however, is to be found in «La compañera» (AP, 265).   For the purpose of defining the poet's relationship with his solitude, he draws on examples from nature which illustrate the marvelously unified and integrated wholes formed by the universe. Similes such as «. . . como la mar junto a los pinos . . . y el cielo con la tierra . . .» serve to stress the «rightness» of his oneness with solitude. Completed and strengthened by this union («. . . Lo uno con lo otro tan cerrado/ que se completa la mitad que falta . . .»), the poet readies himself for his spiritual journey: «. . . y ya todo está bien. No importa nada./ No importa el ruido, ni la ciudad, ni la máquina./ No te importa. . . .» The ultimate significance of solitude as a trampoline from which the soul springs to the ineffable union with God is revealed in the poem's concluding verse:

> A veces se la encuentra
> en mitad del camino de la vida
> y ya todo está bien.   No importa nada.
> No importa el ruido, ni la ciudad, ni la máquina.
> No te importa.   La llevas de la mano
> --compañera tan fiel como la muerte--
> y así va con el tren como el paisaje,
> en el aire de abril como la primavera,
> como la mar junto a los pinos,
> junto a la loma como está la palma,
> o el chopo junto al río,
> o aquellos arrayanes junto al agua.
> No importa.   Como todo lo que une
> y completa.   Junto a la sed el agua,
> y al dolor, el olvido.   El fuego con la fragua,
> la flor y la hoja verde,
> y el mar azul y la espuma blanca.
> La niña pequeñita
> con el brazo de amor que la llevaba,
> y el ciego con su perro lazarillo,
> y el Tormes junto a Salamanca.
> Lo uno con lo otro tan cerrado
> que se completa la mitad que falta.
> y el cielo con la tierra.
> Y el cuerpo con el alma
> Y tú, por fin, para decirlo pronto,
> mi soledad, en Dios, transfigurada.

These writings, then certify the belief that man's reach for transcendence is essentially a solitary undertaking: only in radical solitude can contact be made with God.

Transcendence: A Variety of Perspectives

The ineffability of God implies that he cannot be enmeshed in concepts or understood by a process of analysis, separation, or resynthesis. His truth is apprehended by sudden «revelation» though it is not to be had without the prior rigorous process of thought. Reason and rapture are really complementary: the one is needed to drive and lift, the other to control and guide.

As viewed by existential thinkers, man can, by virtue of his ideality, tug at the moorings of his finitude and transcend the time-space world. Man is the Heideggerian «ecstatic» being who stands at a distance from himself or he is, in the language of Sartre, a being not only «in himself» (as immediately present in what he does) but «for himself» (as transcending his own actuality). It is principally from an existential perspective that transcendence is described in «Extraña luz» (AP, 214) and «Momento de cielo» (AP, 177). The first of these two poems abstractly encapsulates in its first two stanzas the essence of the Heideggerian state. Just as the poet's thoughts, by virtue of enjambement, are not held captive by the constriction of the verse line, so does the soul, momentarily detached from the disquiet of temporal existence, engage dispassionately in auto-contemplation:

¡Qué luz tan extraña
la del alma
cuando está sola en la casa
y se mira llorar
desde fuera de sus lágrimas!

¡Qué extraña luz extraña
a todo, a su cerrada
tristeza, a su terror
de llamarse sin ver
cómo le salen las palabras! . . .

The re-entry from transcendence to facticity is posited in the last stanza and is punctuated strategically by the introduction of the comma as signifier of material restraint:

> . . . ¡Y qué luz más extraña
> la que vuelve cansada
> y se pone a dormir, tímida,
> en el borde amarillo
> de la lámpara!

What we encounter again in «Momento de cielo» is a consciously ecstatic state wherein the distinction between subject and object (the soul and God) and the opposition between subject and subject (the body and the soul) are not fully transcended. It has been suggested by Stace that mystical illumination is infinite in itself because there is nothing outside it, because within it «there is no this or that, no limiting otherness.»(9) «Momento de cielo,» on the other hand, while purporting to look at transcendence from within the experience itself remains inextricably tied to a consciousness of a time-space order, as revealed in the poem's title.(10) Hence the acosmism of mysticism is not present. Rather, at work here is the discriminating intellect, the self-awareness of transcendence as understood by existentialist writers. The ecstatic state, labeled only in the final stanza, is arrived at by the exercise of the intellect with reason serving as the handmaiden of the spirit: «. . . Su éxtasis de hombre junto al cielo,/ a la entrada de Dios,/ frente a la puerta libre y ancha/ de su más noble pensamiento.» It is not necessary to make one's way to these final assertions, however, to encounter an explicit awareness of reflexive consciousness and polarity. It makes itself felt straightaway in the poem's opening verses («Y desde allí miró:/ su cuerpo descansaba en sueño largo»), and in subsequent allusions («. . . Pero desde la altura . . . se veía en lo hondo. . . . Pero, desde él, desde la altura . . .»).

The poem's title, «Momento de cielo,» which suggests that eternal truth is glimpsed in a temporal moment, immediately offsets opposing concepts that define existence as dialectical process. Man's finite self, tied to the body and the senses, and subject to imperfections is located in a time-space world:

... *Allí sí, abajo revolaban* — (This self is positioned «below» in opposition to a celestial realm

dentro y sobre su cuerpo — (It is subject to internal and external temptation)

Los dardos con su punta,
los agudos cuchillos; — (The pains, wants, and cravings tied to the sensible, mutable self)

Los deseo allí, con su pequeño
círculo de palabras y suspiros. — (The circular, hence, unending signs of the language of appetition)

Time's flux, expressed metaphorically through changing images of light (sunset, twilight, nightfall) is tied to the finite self alone, and stands in contrast to the «eternal sun» of a transcendent realm:

> ... *Y qué color de rojos a sus pies,*
> *de amarillo y violeta del ocaso,*
> *de grises, de jirones áureos;*
> *y después, a la ausencia momentánea*
> *del sol para su cuerpo en tierra,*
> *los azulados tintes y las sombras*
> *como unos pensamientos oscuros de la luna.*
>
> *Pero desde él, desde la altura,*
> *la sombra de allá abajo parecía,*
> *un color que se muda entre dos puntos,*
> *entre el ya y el aún: el impreciso*
> *resbalar de la luz por la penumbra* ...

Yet, by virtue of his ideality, man can transcend the concrete world, moving into the nothingness where the great light is («. . . con él ahora estaba/ el azul-negro y la total ausencia . . .»). The ascension to a celestial realm of pure forms is concretized by spatial imagery («. . . desde la altura,/ hermano de las nubes, asomado/ a una esquina del cielo . . .»).

With transcendence comes the repudiation of facticity («. . .

su cuerpo descansaba . . . inútil con su sangre indiferente . . . como veía inútil/ desde su altura el cuerpo . . .»), the identification of the authentic self as unrelated to the body («. . . Pero desde él, desde la altura . . .») and an escape from the contingency of time («. . . Estar así, donde se juntan/ los días y las noches . . .»).   The freedom alluded to with the verse «. . . Libre, solo y etéreo . . . ,» may be interpreted in an existential sense as free choice and self-direction, or both Platonically and mystically as liberation from the body.   The poem, moreover, draws an ontological-ontic distinction; that between man's finite being and Absolute Being.   While God as the absolute is altogether «other» than man's world, man can, in his ecstatic state, transcend his finitude and perceive his immutable light: «. . . Ahora cerca del sol eterno,/ cerca de Dios, cerca de nieves puras,/ en la deslumbra-dora Presencia transformado. . . .»   Apparently infused by His presence, the poet appears to experience a *redintegratio ad statum pristinum* and with it an erasure of all worldly traces:

> . . . *Delicia era*
> *de saberse más alto que el dolor,*
> *puro sobre su cieno,*
> *tranquilo ya sobre sus lágrimas,*
> *grande sobre su amor de tierra,*
> *firme sobre columna de aire y nubes . . .*

Yet, in the final analysis, the absence of total loss of self, indicates that the poet falls short of mystical union.   The rise and fall, the push and pull of opposite forces are ever present in the corpus of the poem and are expressed in the poetic praxis.   The poem is, in fact, a complex organization of antithesis and repetitions which by their very presence form a spatial structure embodying the poet's message.   A schematic study of the topology of the poem reveals a marked imbalance between heaven and earth-related images and thus adduces persuasive evidence that the poet indeed finds himself «a la entrada de Dios» (Table 1).

However, the preponderance of ascensional images is not complemented by a similar imbalance where temporal images are concerned.   The pull between a mutable and an immutable realm is almost equalized numerically (Table 2).   Other antitheses further exasperate the sense of dichotimization:

TABLE I

Spatial   Imagery

Heaven	Earth
1. Desde allí #1	1. Se veía en lo hondo aprisionado #7
2. Desde la altura #4	2. Allí sí, abajo # 14
3. No era mirar la altura #27	3. los deseos allí # 18
4. Desde su altura #42	4. Y qué color de rojos a sus pies # 43
5. Desde la altura #50	5. para su cuerpo en tierra # 47
6. Desde él #50	6. la sombra de allá abajo # 51
7. hermano de las nubes #5	7. ¿Dónde aquella mirada? #11
8. con él sobre las nubes # 21	8. ¿Dónde la lágrima? # 12
9. sobre columna de aire y nubes # 33	9. ¿Dónde el triste pensamiento # 12-13
10. Asomado a una esquina del cielo # 5-6	
11. asomado/ a una esquina del cielo # 23-24	
12. cerca del sol eterno # 24	
13. cerca de Dios # 25	
14. cerca de nieves puras # 25	
15. junta al cielo # 56	
16. Pero los sueños, qué altos # 20	
17. de saberse más alto # 29	

TABLE I [continued]

Heaven	Earth
18. Alto, para estar libre # 39	
19. Sobre las nubes # 21	
20. estaba sobre él # 28	
21. puro sobre su cieno # 30	
22. tranquilo ya sobre sus lágrimas # 31	
23. grande sobre su amor # 32	
24. firme sobre columna de aire y nubes # 33	
25. Donde su juntan/ los días y las noches # 34-35	
26. Donde al pensar se encienden más estrellas # 36	
27. Donde se sueña, y nace Dios # 37	
28. Donde Dios ha nacido en nuestro sueño # 38	

TABLE II

Temporal Images

The Eternal	The Temporal
1. Cuando en él ahora estaba/ el azul-negro y la total ausencia # 9-10	1. Y qué color de rojos a sus pies/ de amarillo y violeta del ocaso # 43-44
2. Ahora en él sobre las nubes # 21	2. Sombra de allá abajo # 51
3. Ahora cerca del sol eterno # 24	3. entre el ya y el aún # 54
4. tranquilo ya # 31	4. el impreciso/ resbalar de la luz por la penumbra # 53-54
5. Donde se juntan los días y las noches # 34-35	

1. Puro--cieno # 30
2. tranquilo--lágrimas # 31
3. tierra # 32--columna de aire # 33
4. color de rojos # 43--el azul-negro # 10
5. dolor-risa # 8--la total ausencia # 10
6. sol eterno # 24--ausencia . . . del sol # 46-47
7. su cuerpo descansaba en sueño largo # 2--sueño del sueño # 55
8. los deseos . . . con su pequeño círculo # 18-19--Libre, solo, etéreo # 40
9. en la deslumbradora Presencia # 26--a la entrada de Dios # 57

Thus, the assertion of a principle of unification over one of distinction is never fully realized. A quintessential expression of the ecstatic state, «Momento de cielo» suggests but then denies the total lift of rapture.

A direct *scientia visionis,* understood Platonically, is experienced and evoked in the poem «Ya silencio» (AP, 79). Looked at from outside the moment itself, transcendence, whose metaphoric carrier is «silence,» becomes datable as a specific point in time («. . . al regresar de este minuto de silencio . . . en el minuto ausente . . .»). Descrying Supreme Reality, the poet is lifted above mutability, enlightened and free: «. . . Cuerpo de carne y de tierra, prendido hasta ayer en la/ sombra que se va cada tarde,/ ya libre en el vuelo, con la ciencia de un solo resplandor de/ silencio. . . .» In his *scientia visionis* the poet apprehends and learns eternal truths:

Ahora, encerrado en un minuto de silencio
--mejor aún: al regresar de este minuto de silencio--,
puede contarse cómo corren los vientos sobre todos los
mares
y cómo suena la voz ya desnuda, y el aliento que vuela
sin rumbo.
Se sabe que el ayer está vivo junto al hoy y al mañana
--tres hojitas de trébol en la mano dormida de Dios--:
que la canción puesta a volar sin destino seguro
aún agita sus alas por las esquinas abiertas del cielo;
y que el perfume y la llama que murieron de frío
tienen un paraíso de flores y almas rojas con élitros rubios;
y que todo el amor está de pie bajo la luz de las estrellas
con el beso que salió de unos labios en el suspiro último;

y se sabe también adónde va el polvo de las mariposas
y en qué rincón del mundo se tiñen de azul los ojos de los
ángeles
Todo esto, aprendido en el minuto ausent, con el asombro
entre los labios,
habrá de estar latiendo ya para siempre . . .

Through transcendence, the mind apprehends wholes and functions synoptically rather than analytically; it is noetic not discursive «. . . No, ya no hay que gritar, sintiéndose en el centro de este mundo.» Similarly, the confluence of the three dimensions of time suggests an eternal «now,» a *nunc stans* in which all uncertainties are resolved into inward peace gained through the vision of the Immutable One: «. . . Se sabe que el ayer está vivo junto al hoy y el mañana/ --tres hojitas de trébol en la mano dormida de Dios--. . . .» In a Pythagorean and Platonic sense, the mind comes to grasp cosmic order and harmony: «. . . Beber ahora el silencio donde las músicas escondieron sus alas/ para ser armonía de siglos en el laberinto de las/ constelaciones. . . . Donde se escucha aquella música puesta sin pauta en el/ espacio. . . .» The perception of Platonic forms, disembodied and pure, is possible within the experience of attainment («. . . un recuerdo de perfume, ausente de/ su clavel desvanecido . . . era tan firme el color y tan pura la palabra . . .»).

The difficulty of communicating what is essentially an incommunicable experience is translated into the poetic praxis. The compelling desire to capture the experience while it is still fresh is conveyed by the bursting verse lines (fifteen to nineteen syllables), the lengthy stanzas (forty-two verses), the absence of rhyme, the frequent use of enjambement, all suggesting the need to record feelings straightaway and without pause. Words are as grappling irons let down into the depth of the subconscious and surface as poetic images which shape and give substance to ineffable feeling. The abstract is frequently personified in an effort to render it comprehensible and real («. . . la canción agita sus alas . . . el perfume y la llama que murieron de frío . . . el amor está de pie . . . donde la músicas escondieron sus alas . . .»)

The topographic definition of transcendence of the second stanza makes manifest the hope that once the course is charted, it will be possible to travel it again and again: «. . . Allí, allí. Donde aún agita sus cabellos el aire./ Desde donde nos llega un

recuerdo de perfume. . . . Donde se escucha aquella música. . . .
Oh, sí es allí . . . en ese punto de la noche. . . . Allí, allí. Más
lejos del corazón desierto de la hormiga,/ más lejos de tu asombro
ante una flor recién puesta en el agua. . . .» The integrative
nature of transcendence, its wholeness, is suggested tropistically
through the use of synesthesia («. . . Beber el silencio . . . un solo
resplandor de silencio . . .») and by the union of the spatial and the
temporal («. . . encerrado en un minuto . . .») which reaches
its ripest meaning at the poem's end («. . . Ya solo había que estar
con el silencio entre las manos/ desde allí, desde siempre . . .»).
The transcendent vision etches with a new clarity the ineffable
sense of the wonder, beauty, and unity of the Ultimate.

If «Ya silencio» is essentially ontological in its perspective,
in «Variaciones sobre un verso de Fray Diego de Hojeda» (AP,
338) the soul is described as having got beyond «science» itself
to a full realization of God. Apprehension in no longer «knowing
about» but is, instead, an actual possession-of and being pos-
sessed-by. The concepts of «Beauty,» «Truth,» or «Good» to
which the soul is mated in classic writings is translated here into
the *ens realissimum* of Christian philosophers. The poet testifies
retrospectively to an experience of ecstatic union with God in
which the very distinctions between *esse* and *essentia* appear to
fall away. The feeling he experiences is «singular»: free of
self-reflective complexities, it involves the direct reaction of inner
emotion on outer experience («. . . Así de esta manera singular/
que no sabemos quién lo piensa, o cuándo . . .»). The poem
carries us from rapturous flight (Stanza I) to union and renewed
desire (Stanza II) to the postulation of permanent union through
death and enlightened acquiescence (Stanza III). However, the
accent of the poem falls primarily on the difficulties of predicating
and communicating the poet's mystic experience. While the
numinous is felt as ineffable and therefore not susceptible to
conceptualization, the poet nonetheless seeks some analogues
within the natural world (daybreak, the wind, night, water). Yet,
the entire poem hangs on the assertion-denial of «Así, pero no
así» (reiterated ten times) which bespeaks the essential incom-
municability of the experience. Nowhere is this more apparent
than in the poem's first section (seven stanzas) which, in its
attempt to describe the rapturous, soaring aloft of the love-struck
soul serves as a paradigm of the difficulties therein. The poet's
«vuelo,» the subject of the entire section is qualified by a series of

comparisons that tend to form natural groups:

A
1. Así, pero no así, I, #1
2. Así, II, # 1
3. Pero no así, III, # 1
4. pero no así, V, # 1
5. Así, VI, # 1
6. Pero no así, VI, # 1

B

1. con mayor vuelo, I, # 1
2. más firme, III, # 1
3. más seguro, III, # 1
4. con mayor vuelo, IV, # 1
5. vuelo mayor, V, # 1
6. más alto, V, # 1
7. más limpio, V, # 3
8. más audaz, V, # 3
9. con mayor salto, V, # 3
10. más, VI, # 1
11. más así, VI, # 1
12. más cierto, VI, # 1
13. más, VII, # 1
14. siempre más, VII, # 1
15. vibrando más, VII, # 2
16. más alto, VII, # 2

C

1. Como suben los claros pensamientos, I, # 2
2. Como la aurora sube por el cielo, I, # 3
3. como en la tarde lánzase el cantar, II, # 3
4. mayor vuelo que los serafines, IV, # 1
5. Vuelo mayor . . . que el agua, V, # 1-2
6. más cierto/ que la espada cimera de la palma, VI, # 1-2

The upward sweep of the soul is mirrored in the poetic praxis:

A. Verbs

1. Como suben los claros pensamientos, I, # 2
2. como la aurora sube, I, # 3
3. al remontarse en alas, I, # 4
4. lánzase, II, # 3
5. cruzan sobre los trémulos confines, IV, # 3
6. salirse, V, # 2
7. lanza su flecha, V, # 4

B. Nouns

1. cielo, I, # 3
2. alas, I, # 4
3. altura, II, # 4
4. noche estrellada, III, # 4
5. vuelo, IV, # 1
6. serafines, IV, # 1
7. vuelo, V, # 1
8. salto, V, # 3
9. flecha, V, # 4
10. *espada* cimera de la *palma*, VI, # 2
11. Al *aire* ofrece el *pico* de su alma, VI, # 4
12. cielo, VII, # 2

C. Adverbs

1. Allá (en la altura), II, # 4

D. Adjectives

1. alto, V, # 1
2. alto, VII, # 2

E. Prepositions

1. sobre, IV, # 3

The multiple qualifiers of the noun «vuelo» and the concentrated repetition of the first part of the poem speak, then, to the difficulties of nailing down emotions with precision or accuracy. Repetition, moreover, serves to heighten feeling: the meaning radiated by the comparative, «más» when employed for the twelfth time is not comparable to its relative impact the first time around. A crescendo is clearly reached in the final stanza when mystic and poetic illumination coalesce and meaning emerges, clarified and whole. The correlation between «flight» and «love» is finally made explicit as is the unified purposiveness («tu solo vuelo») of the soul's journey: «Más, siempre más amor. Tu solo vuelo/ vibrando más, más alto por el cielo.» Flowing freely from these verses, love imagery spills over and prevails in the poem's second section. The «amor» of stanza seven, part I, is further personalized and focused as «este amor» of stanza one, part II, and the poet is implicitly identified as «el que ama.» The intensity of the gerund of «vibrar» of part I (7) is matched and surpassed by «apetecer» (5), «anhelar» (7), «encender» (7), and «esperar,» twice repeated (7-8) of part II. The *via unitiva* here is both rapturous flight and colloquy of love. First, the soul intuits and ascends to a supercelestial realm where purity of color connotes value:

> . . . *sube este amor al alto cielo*
> *que tras las nubes se divisa.*
>
> *No el cielo negro, mas celeste*
> *para el que ama y el que sueña;*
> *cielo azul más intenso que este*
> *que la pintura nos enseña . . .*

The dialogue between the beloved and the soul is reserved for a transcendent realm to which entrance is gained by the sheer force of volition and desire, conveyed here by the verbs «taladrar» and «penetrar» to which it is analogized:

> . . . *y por mayor vuelo taladra*
> *los espacios que lo reciben*
> *como penetra la palabra*
> *de las manos que la escriben,*
>
> *y así, pero no así, más honda*
> *deja en la letra su mensaje;*

> *que ya tendrá quien le responda*
> *en el término de su viaje . . .*

With union, all strivings, aspirations, and uncertainties are peacefully resolved. The soul, like the thrush who is drawn to its nest, finds its final resting place within God:

> *. . . Que ya tendrán palabra y vuelo*
> *fin y descanso apetecido*
> *como la alondra cae del cielo*
> *a la llamada de su nido.*

> *Vuelo mayor, sueño que se alienta*
> *y en sólo un nombre se resuelva, . . .*

The mystic illumination acts as a point of intersection between an eternal and temporal order. The mystic poet experiences the one yet soon falls back on the other: «. . . y alza el ala que sube, exenta,/ y bebe su aire y luego vuelve. . . .» He is left to his impassioned longings to experience rapture once more: «. . . Vuelve a soñar con lo que deja/ y a esperar lo que le enciende con la queja/ de pasarse la vida en vela. . . .» The poem's second section again places some reliance on comparisons to capture meaning but does so in a less frenzied and diffuse manner. The poem's refrain «Así, pero no así» is repeated but twice and the number of similes is held down to two («. . . como penetra la palabra . . . como la alondra . . .»). The increased selectivity and distillation of language concords with the emotional catharsis and repose of union. The queries of the poem's third section speak to the longing to resolve permanently the painful dichotimization between opposing realms.

The poem «La noche» (AP, 257) is especially interesting for the light it sheds on mystic attainment as direct communion which cannot be logicized and which therefore defies accepted standards of verification. The prior stages of the soul's preparation are mentioned and then surpassed. They involve the stilling of the reasoning intellect (the «callado pensamiento») in favor of a Kierkegaardian «leap of faith» which places absolute trust in the wisdom, power, and goodness of God. The stars give symbolic substance to the existence of a transcendent realm on which the soul mimetically models its earthly life: «. . . qué clara la escritura . . . que baja de tus abismos . . . y mata la carne y deja/ el alma en su puro hueso.» Yet, neither ascetic self-discipline nor disposition to flight («. . . lo que dicen las estrellas me tiene, Señor, despierto/ a más altas claridades/ a más disparados vuelos . . .») insure attainment. The soul stands within the cross fire of opposing forces: «. . . un no sé de cauteloso,/ un sí sé de goce trémulo/ (alas de una mariposa/ agitadas por el suelo). . . .» The resolution of this polarity is not effected until the partnership of reason and desire («. . . qué clara la escritura/ dentro de la noche, dentro/ del corazón anheloso/ de recibir este fuego . . .») gives way to the preeminence of desire which requires no mediation to arrive at communion with God. Then, without further pause, the soul's rapturous flight is expressed in a series of incandescent metaphors which culminate in a climactic arrival at «love»: «. . . Paloma de las estrellas/ ala en aire, flecha, hierro/ en el blanco de la fragua/ de tu amor. . . .» The soul's contemporaneity and immediacy with God are invested with the translucent brightness habitually associated with apprehension:

> *En el desvelo*
> *de tantas luces agudas*
> *todo va lejos, huyendo.*
> *Todo, menos Tú, Señor.*
> *Que ya sé cómo me hablas*
> *por las estrellas del cielo.*

Again in «El nuevo San Sebastian» (AP, 220) love is the self-sufficient instrument leading to union with God. While God's positive being is hidden from the intellect it is revealed through intuition: it can only be disclosed when rationality is suffused and transfigured by love:

> *. . . ¡Y el pensar, y el perdido pensamiento*
> *Ya para tu visión enardecido,*
> *hecho de Ti, en tu esencia*
> *y en tu sueño de amor transfigurado . . .*

> *Venga, sí, por silencio y por belleza,*
> *tu dardo rojo al corazón dolido*
> *y clave en amor, donde*

están los pensamientos más oscuros
su rayo estremecido . . .

The transference to a rapturous state is expressed figuratively through the central image of the arrow which, like Cupid's sweet barb, pierces the heart with love. Both the nature of this love and its effect on the smitten soul is described in the fiery language of desire:

A. The heat and color of passion: tactile images of love

1. tu ardor, I, #3
2. el alma de tu fuego, I, #3
3. la luz/ que en hondos rayos atraviesa el alma, I, #4-5
4. (tu voz) la flecha de oro, II, # 1
5. hiere/ con tan herida suave, II, # 3-4
6. tan suave herida tuya, II, # 4
7. al beso de tus flechas, III, # 3-4
8. tu sueño de amor, III, # 8
9. Venga otra vez tu flecha/ ahora de sol, IV, # 1-2
10. el ardoso Tú, III, # 3
11. el silencio de tus oceanos, IV, # 6
12. Venga sí . . . por silencio y por belleza/ tu dardo rojo, IV, # 7-8
13. Clave en amor . . . su rayo estremecido, IV, # 9

B. Its effect on the beloved: smitten, he «sees,» is «illuminated» and surrenders his total being to God («ojos,» «sangre,» «mano,» «pecho,» «pensamiento») clamoring for the arrow anew («Venga otra vez la flecha»).

1. Flechado . . .por tu belleza, I, # 1
2. atado en aire, I, #2
3. mira tu ardor, I, # 3
4. al llegar ahoga, I, # 10
5. te mira estremecido, I, # 11
6. lo oscuro a la firme pasión se le ilumina, II, # 4-5
7. están los ojos en el cielo, II, # 7
8. que la sangre va en ríos/ de amor, II, # 9
9. y estas manos que te señalan, III, # 1
10. y este pecho, Señor, desnudo al beso/ de tus flechas, III,

156

The oxymoronic «a Tí, sombra de luz» of stanza III suggests the double depiction of the eternal Godhead both as the hidden darkness of nonbeing and as the embodiment of true light.   Moreover, the repeated invocation of His silence («. . . por el silencio de tus oceanos/ Venga sí, por silencio y por belleza . . .») is reminiscent of Meister Eckart's «wordless» Godhead.   Attainment, described in stanza I as a form of drowning (al llegar ahoga) is sought again («Venga otra vez») as, in the metaphoric dark night, the soul navigates toward a water union: «. . . el ardoroso Tú, trémulo al aire/ que suena al solo acorde/ con que navega, tímida, la noche/ por el silencio de tus oceanos. . . .»   No intermediaries are needed in this mystic union other than the soul's desire and divine grace: «. . . un hombre, por tu gracia/ aquí, Señor, te mira estremecido.»

It is in the poem «Que estás en los cielos» (AP, 223) that the philosophy of absolute unity and the confluence of love, poetry, and metaphysics reaches its most impassioned expression.   The synoptic nature of apprehension is again emphasized.   Unlike the fragmented perception of God of the state prior to union («. . . Te vi la tarde de la tempestad. . . . Te vi otra tarde, azul . . . entre el verde con frío del arroyo . . .»), mysticism has the character of wholeness: «. . . Si, pero aquella noche . . . Aquella noche, el verte/ fue como ver el Universo entero . . . era una sola luz. . . .»   The psychological experience of union, the lift of the human psyche into ecstasy is transmuted to a purely poetic plane. The soul's cognition of its insignificance, as it is overpowered and possessed by God is expressed through a series of similes: «. . . Fue como estarse frente a Tí,/ desnuda el alma --tan pequeño/ como la luz de la luciérnaga,/ tímido como un ciervo del camino. . . .»   Ineffable love is expressed metaphorically and with an erotic vehemence that reaches almost unbearable tension: «. . . era/ un ansia de llorar pegado a tu belleza;/ de recostarse sobre el suelo,/ de, hasta cegar, estar mirándote. . . .»   In a total surrender to feeling, and in a language reminiscent of San Juan de la Cruz, the soul, smitten by God's beauty, is infused with His light.   The anaphoric «era(n),» repeated four times, reflects the difficulties of translating experience to language:

> . . . *Eran tantas las luces,*
> *era una sola luz que aún en pedazos*
> *ardía--eran millones de besos que besaban.*
> *Y más que todo, era*
> *un ansia de llorar pegado a tu belleza;*
> *de recostarse sobre el suelo,*
> *de, hasta cegar, estar mirándote*
> *y meter tanta luz dentro del alma*
> *--pura en lo oscuro, como las estrellas--*
> *para que nunca me faltara luz*
> *ni Tú ya nunca me faltaras.*

Thus, the unified self the poet cannot always find in nature or in flight from human nature, the self he cannot earn for himself he first receives when he abandons it to God.

A final review of the poems studied under transcendence suggests the following thoughts. When understood existentially, transcendence is arrived at through the exercise of the poet's ideality. Yet, in his ec-static state, Florit as existential thinker resists the voluntary loss of self within the infinite ocean of divine being. Rather, existential insight is chiefly directed toward the conscious engagement in self-realization and self-maintenance.

In a Socratic sense, Florit also testifies in various poems that human reason is invested with the potency to transcend itself. Yet he nonetheles acknowledges that supreme knowledge can only be won through direct «revelation.»

When touched by mystic illumination, the poet eschews reason and moves beyond the Platonic *scientia visionis*. His soul passes from its dark night into the being of God and knows Him in the fullness of His reality (the *ens realissimum* of Christian theology). Yet, while mystic illumination is infinite and eternal when viewed internally, looked at from the outside it is but a moment in time and the unity experienced is but a fragile, transient state. The poet, perforcedly, is returned to a temporal order and with it to a renewal of the struggle for the acceptance and faith that can salvage victory from defeat:

> . . .¡*Ay, el velar de lo que ayer*
> *puso el alma en su mayor vuelo*
> *y el esperar a volver a ver*
> *otra vez el color del cielo. . . .*

Y así, pues hay que ser, he de rendirme
a ser como tú quieras:
hombre tenaz que siente el mayor vuelo
y se afirma a la tierra. (AP, 340-341)

Notes

1. Examples, taken at random, of reduced foci: «Esa esquina de risa» (AP, 62); «. . . en qué rincón del mundo» (AP, 79); «. . . en ese punto de la noche» (AP, 80); «. . . metido en un rincón» (AP, 88); «. . . cerca del punto suave» (AP, 93); «. . . hacia una esquina clara» (AP, 93); «. . . un ángulo del alma» (AP, 225); «. . . un cielo pequeño» (AP, 269); «. . . en esta gota de tu firmamento y en esta esquina de tu clara vida» (AP, 286); «. . . nuestro rincón de vida» (AP, 216).

2. See María Castellanos Collins' *Tierra, mar y cielo en la poesía de Eugenio Florit* (Miami: Ediciones Universal, Colección Polymita, 1976).

3. William Wordsworth, «The Prelude,» book eight, *Selected Poems and Sonnets* (New York and Toronto: Rhinehart and Co., 1959), p. 335.

4. See Orlando E. Saa's *La serenidad en la obra de Eugenio Florit* (Miami: Ediciones Universal, Colección Polymita, 1973) for an interesting analysis of spiritual content and dimension in Florit's poetry.

5. Martin Buber, *Eclipse of God* (New York: Harper, 1952), pp. 27-28.

6. A. N. Whitehead, *Science and the Modern World* (New York: The Macmillan Co., 1954), p. 275.

7. Soren Kierkegaard, *Training in Christianity* (Princeton: Princeton University Press, 1947), pp. 124-127/

8. Ralph Waldo Emerson, «Self Reliance,» Essays First Series, *The Complete Works*, Centenary Edition, ed. Edward Waldo Emerson (Boston: Houghton, Mifflin and Co., 1903), II, pp. 53-54.

9. W. T. Stace, *Time and Eternity: An Essay in the Philosophy of Religion* (Princeton: Princeton University Press, 1952), p. 76.

10. See José Olivio Jiménez' «Un momento definitivo en la poesía de Eugenio Florit,» *Boletín de la Academia Cubana de la Lengua*, X, núms. 3, 4 (julio-diciembre, 1961).

CHAPTER V

CONCLUSION

In Florit's polyphonic writings shaped from various and, at times, dissonant counterpoints, the poet's *cantus firmus* flows from an acknowledgment of the polarity and paradox that inhere at every stage of human existence. His opus confirms man's status in reality as that of an «inter-esse» involving incessant struggle «between» being and becoming, chaos and cosmos, disquiet and serenity, mortality and eternity. The Janus-like view of Eros(1) and Thanatos,(2) of a Nature which alternately bespeaks the descendental or transcendental, life in permanent mutation or in permanent duration, merely attests to the ambiguity that characterizes human nature. No one feature can be said to be more essential than any other for each is an equal part of the poet's totality as a unitary being and clamors equally for recognition and attention. Each, alone and together, bespeaks the battle being pitched between Florit as essential philosopher viewing life *sub specie aeternitatis* on the one hand, and as an existential thinker grappling daily with the paradoxes of life on the other. Chronology, as noted earlier, has no bearing on this battle which is waged every step of the way. It may reveal itself in sequential or contemporaneous writings, in discrete collections or one, across different poems or within the same, in several verses(3) or by a single line(4) or title.(5) In given poems, opposing thoughts may even be offset in two parts of equal weight with the second carrying disclaimers of the ideas expressed in the first.(6) Whatever its shape, it is the reality of this polarity that acts as the principal motor of Florit's poetry. The bifurcations of mood, perception, and voice merely confirm this truth and attest that poetic unicity does not mean univocality.

Yet, while the poet's nature is woven from a skein of contradictions representing various values and levels of insight, his many writings nonetheless exhibit a common root: the quest for a harmony through which these difference may be resolved, reconciled, or endured. To this end, in the course of his writing, he has exerted distinct levels of control: the formalism of «pure» poetry with its emphasis on precision of style, the poet's aesthetic of salvation; the idealizing activity of the imagination and the intellect which, in accordance with the demands of the will reshape the world depicted by the senses--as in *Trópico;* the tempering of passion through abstraction, distancing, and indirection--studied under Eros; the choice of noninvolvement (freedom suspended from decision) or death-as-a-way-of-life, examined under Thanatos; the imaginative revision of the past of an *art of recollection* and, most centrally, the exaltation of a beneficent nature, the laws of Reason, and the lessons of Faith. The poet, indeed, experiences periods of integration and stability when he knows himself whole. Yet, what harmonious unity Florit encounters and by whatever means (love, nature, God) the synthesis of opposites it presupposes is, at best, a fragile state and carries within it the seeds of its own dissolution, for in the poet's temporal existence, the laws of contradiction and polarity cannot be permanently abrogated.

Yet, in sudden visitations of lucidity, Florit finds the strength to accept the certainty of defeat in life and of victory in death. His resolve lies with the affirmation and seizure of the meaning of life as a rehearsal for dying and of death as completion and oneness with the Supreme Good of both Hellenic and mystic thought. Death alone becalms the tensions of body and soul, the rise and fall of reason and rapture:

> . . . *¿Cuándo, Señor, el mayor vuelo*
> *dejará en nuestros labios,*
> *con la ausencia de trémulos ardores,*
> *el beso sin color de los espacios?*
>
> *¿Cuándo, por fin, este deseo*
> *de acompañar la soledad,*
> *ha de caer, y así, pero no así,*
> *podamos empezar*
>
> *a tomar otra vez el vuelo*
> *que nos remonta al alto*
> *dominio del Amor, sin esta angustia*

de dónde, y cómo, y cuándo? . . . (AP, 340)

Pasan las gentes con su risa
con sus pequeñas lágrimas oscuras.
Gracias, Señor,
por verlas desde lejos, de la altura.

De la altura se ven con sus palabras,
con sus brazos de amor en la cintura . . .
Perdóname, Señor,
este deseo de bajar desde la altura;

este deseo de dejar el cielo
de un momento de paz segura.
Tú lo sabes: después
habrá de nuevo el anhelar la altura.

(Hasta que un día, el único entre todos,
me dejes con el alma por la altura.) (AP, 232)

In «El viaje» (1918-1951, AP, 295), returning to his beloved water imagery, Florit allows that man's existential baggage, his «inquietud» can be deposited ashore when the sea of life is traded for a sea of death:

. . . Este mar es el mismo
que aquel ardiente mar:
un verano me trajo
y otro me llevará.

Las orillas distintas
al salir y al llegar.
Si distinto el deseo
es la inquietud igual.

Las aguas que me llevan
ya me devolverán.
Hasta que llegue el día
del absoluto mar.

Through death the soul can, at last, effect its escape from the fortunes of the body and lift itself above mutability and corruption («libre del tiempo»)(7) to a divine realm in which it will participate fully and whole. The longing for this supreme knowledge is given magisterial expression in «Martirio de San Sebastian» as the following extrapolated verses reveal:

[*The arrows*]

> . . . *Venid a mis ojos, que puedan ver la luz;*
> *a mis manos, que toquen forma imperecedera;*
> *a mis oídos, que se abran a las aéreas músicas;*
> *a mi boca, que guste las mieles infinitas;*
> *a mi nariz, para el perfume de las eternas rosas.*
> *Venid, sí, duros ángeles de fuego,*
> *pequeños querubines de alas tensas.*
> *Si, venid, a soltarme las amarras*
> *para lanzarme al viaje sin orillas* . . . (AP, 91)

Death is viewed, then, as full fruition («. . . Ya está bien Señor . . .»)(8) where, in absence from life's sorrow («. . . Este largo morir despedazado/ cómo me ausenta del dolor . . .»),(9) the soul can come to final rest («. . . ¿Cuándo podremos/ respirar en un aire/ en el que todo nuestro ser/ con fiel amor descanse? . . .»(10) «Ay, que poco me falta para verte,/ hora de paz, silencio verdadero/ generosa caricia de la muerte»).(11) Death, therefore, should be met head-on, with all defenses down:

> . . . *Cuando sea el momento quiero verla*
> *para darle, despierto, el alma.* (AP, 186)

> *Fuego tuyo callado, música pura;*
> *para sentir el beso marcho desnudo,*
> *en olvido la espada, roto el escudo,*
> *convertida en jirones mi vestidura.*

> *Ya se me acerca el filo de tus puñales;*
> *ya para abrirme el alma cómo te asomas*
> *en ese vuelo trémulo de las palomas*
> *a beber la amargura de mis cristales.* (AP, 118)

In following Eugenio Florit through his long and difficult

quest it seems clear that though absolute harmony stands beyond his finite achievement, the poet is fully sustained by belief in the deiformity of the soul and by the hope of receiving himself, in death, as an in-dividuum at last:

> *Y aquí donde me tienes, noche, sin movimiento,*
> *mirándome las manos que olvidaron el color de su boca,*
> *aquí puedo sellarme la canción,*
> *ya mudo, solo y uno, en isla exacta,*
> *para fijar estrellas a mi caudal de sangre*
> *detenido a la sombra de tu música.* (AP. 119)

Notes

1. Eros as the tendance of the body and Eros as the tendance of the soul.
2. Death as adversary and as liberator. The «dying life» and death-as-a-way-of-life.
3. The opposition of body and soul expressed in several verses: «Hombre, Señor, frente a la luz . . ./ y si quiere volar se amarra al suelo/ y cae, de cansado, en el abismo» («El nuevo San Sebastián,» AP, 270).
4. Nature as flux and as permanence in one verse: «Agua errante y fija» («Homenaje a Goethe,» AP, 101).
5. Acoustical oppositions: «Canción del silencio,» AP, 73; temporal oppositions: «Viejos versos de hoy,» AP, 96; «Tarde presente,» AP, 171).
6. «Cierto que . . . sí; pero a pesar de todo,» acts as a line of demarcation for the two sections of «Pensamientos en un día de sol,» AP, 315, and «Lo que escribí, bien sabes que es retórica» for those of «El resignado,» DTA, 57.
7. «Al unicornio» (AP, 142).
8. «Martirio de San Sebastián» (AP, 92).
9. *Ibid.*
10. «Variaciones sobre un verso de Fray Diego de Hojeda» (AP, 340).
11. «Casi soneto» (AP, 134).

165

BIBLIOGRAPHY

I

EUGENIO FLORIT

«Una hora conmigo», *Revista Cubana,* VII, núms. 4, 5, 6 (1935), 97-108.

«Regreso a la serenidad,» *Universidad de la Habana,* III, núms. 8-9 (marzo-junio, 1935), 97-108.

Antología penúltima. Madrid: Editorial Plenitud, 1970. (Poems, 1930-1970, with a preliminary study by José Olivio Jiménez.)

De tiempo y agonía (Versos del hombre solo). Madrid: Revista de Occidente, 1974.

II

Other Works Cited

Alonso, Amado. *Materia y forma en poesía.* Madrid: Gredos, 1965.

Alonso, Dámaso. *Estudio y ensayos gongorinos.* Madrid: Gredos, 1955.

—————. *Poetas españoles contemporáneos.* Madrid: Gredos, 1958.

—————. *Poesía española: ensayo de método y límites estilísticos.* Madrid: Gredos, 1966.

—————. «Un poeta y un libro,» *Revista de occidente,* XXIII, núm. 98 (agosto 1931).

Bousoño, Carlos. *Teoría de la expresión poética.* Madrid:

Gredos, 1966.

——————. *La poesía de Vicente Aleixandre.* Madrid: Gredos, 1968.

Brumbaugh, Robert S. *Plato for the Modern Age.* New York: Crowell-Collier Press, 1962.

Buber, Martin. *Eclipse of God; Studies in the Relation Between Religion and philosophy.* New York, Harper: 1952.

Ciplijauskaité, Biruté. *La soledad y la poesía española contemporánea.* Madrid: Insula, 1962.

——————. *El poeta y la poesía, del romanticismo a la poesía social.* Madrid: Insula, 1966.

Debicki, Andrew. *Estudios sobre poesía española contemporánea.* Madrid: Gredos, 1966.

Eliot, Thomas Stearns. *The Use of Poetry and the Use of Criticism.* London: Faber and Faber Ltd., 1950.

Emerson, Ralph Waldo. *Essays First Series, The Complete Works.* Centenary Edition II. Boston: Houghton, Mifflin and Co., 1903

Ewer, Mary Anita. *A Survey of Mystical Symbolism.* New York: the Macmillan Co., 1933.

Fairchild, Hoxie Neale. *The Romantic Quest.* Philadelphia: Saifer, 1931.

Fernández de la Vega, O. «Florit y la evasión trascendente,» *Noverim,* La Habana, V. 2, núm. 8 (mayo, 1958).

Flys, Miguel Jaroslaw. *La poesía existencial de Dámaso Alonso.* Madrid: Gredos, 1968.

Fussell, Paul. *Poetic Metre and Poetic Form.* New York: Random House, 1965.

Guillén, Jorge. *Language and Poetry.* Cambridge, Mass.: Harvard University Press, 1961.

Gullón, Ricardo. *Estudios sobre Juan Ramón Jiménez.* Buenos Aires: Editorial Losada, 1960

Heidegger, Martin. *Existence and Being.* Chicago: H. Regnery, 1960.

Henríquez Ureña, Pedro. *La versificación irregular en la poesía española.* Madrid: Revista de filología española, 1920.

Heraclitus. *The Cosmic Fragments.* Edited with introduction and commentary by G. S. Kirk. Cambridge, England, University Press, 1962.

Jiménez, José Olivio. *Cinco poetas del tiempo.* Madrid: Insula, 1964.

————————. »Un momento definitivo en la poesía de Eugenio
Florit,» *Boletín de la Academia Cubana de la Lengua,* La
Habana, V. X, núms. 3, 4.

————————. «La poesía de Eugenio Florit,» Prologue to *Antología penúltima* of Eugenio Florit. Madrid: Plenitud, 1970.

Jiménez, Juan Ramón. «El único estilo de Eugenio Florit,»
Prologue to *Doble acento* of Eugenio Florit. La Habana:
Ucar García, 1937.

Kayser, Wolfgang. *Interpretación y análisis de la obra literaria.* Madrid: Gredos, 1965.

Kierkegaard, Soren. *Concluding Unscientific Postscript.* Princeton: Princeton University Press, 1944.

————————. *Training in Christianity.* Princeton: Princeton
University Press, 1947.

Lazo, R. «Sobre: Cuatro Poemas,» *Revista Iberoamericana,*
México, núm. 5, 1941.

Mueller, Gustav Emil. *Plato, the Founder of Philosophy as Dialectic.* New York: Philosophical Library, 1965.

Plato. *Phaedo.* Translated with notes by David Gallop.
Oxford, England: Claredon Press, 1975.

————————. *Symposium.* New York: Liberal Arts Press,
1950.

Pollin, Alice. *Concordancias de la obra poética de Eugenio Florit.*
New York: New York University Press, 1967.

Río, Angel del. «La literatura de hoy: Eugenio Florit,» *Revista
Hispánica Moderna,* Madrid, Año 8, núm. 3, 1942.

Saa, Orlando E. *La serenidad en la obra de Eugenio Florit.*
Miami: Ediciones Universal, Colección Polymita, 1973.

Salinas, Pedro. *La poesía de Rubén Darío.* Buenos Aires:
Editorial Losada, 1948.

————————. *Reality and the Poet in Spanish Poetry.* Baltimore:
John Hopkins University Press, 1940.

Sartre, Jean Paul. *L'être et le néant; essai d'ontologie phéno-
ménologique.* Paris: Gallimard, 1966.

Silver, Philip. «*Et in Arcadia Ego*»: *A Study of the Poetry of
Luis Cernuda.* London: Tamesis Books Ltd., 1965.

Stace, W. T. *Time and Eternity: An Essay in the Philosophy of
Religion.* Princeton: Princeton University Press, 1952.

Stiernotte, Alfred P. *Mysticism and the Modern Mind.* New
York: Liberal Arts Press, 1959.

Taylor, Alfred Edward. *Platonism and its Influence.* Boston:

Jones, 1924.

Vitier, C. *Lo cubano en la poesía.* [Santa Clara], Cuba: Universidad Central de las Villas, 1958.

Wellek, R., and Warren, Austin. *Teoría literaria.* Madrid: Gredos, 1967.

Whitehead, Alfred North. *Science and the Modern World.* New York: The Macmillan Co., 1954.

Wordsworth, William. *Selected Poems and Sonnets.* New York: Rhinehart and Co., 1959.

Zardoya, Concha. «Asonante final y otros poemas,» *Revista Hispánica Moderna,* XXIII, núms. 3-4, 1957.

Addenda

The following books have been published since the completion of the manuscript:

Castellanos Collins, María. *Tierra, mar y cielo en la poesía de Eugenio Florit.* Miami: Ediciones Universal, Colección Polymita, 1976.

Parajón, Mario. *Eugenio Florit y su poesía.* Madrid: Insula, 1977.